You're a Good Man, Sergeant

Sergeant Paul S. Porter (Colleen C. Porter family collection).

You're a Good Man, Sergeant

The World War II Combat Memoir of an Armored Infantryman in Patton's Third Army

PAUL S. PORTER

Edited by COLLEEN C. PORTER
with DON M. FOX

McFarland & Company, Inc., Publishers
Jefferson, North Carolina

ALSO OF INTEREST
AND FROM McFARLAND

*Final Battles of Patton's Vanguard:
The United States Army Fourth Armored Division, 1945–1946*
(Don M. Fox, 2020)

*Patton's Vanguard:
The United States Army Fourth Armored Division*
(Don M. Fox, 2003; paperback 2007)

LIBRARY OF CONGRESS CATALOGUING-IN-PUBLICATION DATA

Names: Porter, Paul S., 1923–1985, author. | Porter, Colleen C., 1953– editor. | Fox, Don M., 1958–
Title: You're a good man, sergeant : the World War II combat memoir of an armored infantryman in Patton's Third Army / Paul S. Porter ; edited by Colleen C. Porter, with Don M. Fox.
Other titles: World War II combat memoir of an armored infantryman in Patton's Third Army
Description: Jefferson, North Carolina : McFarland & Company, Inc., Publishers, 2024 | Includes bibliographical references and index.
Identifiers: LCCN 2024032548 | ISBN 9781476695709 (paperback : acid free paper) ∞ ISBN 9781476653730 (ebook)
Subjects: LCSH: Porter, Paul S., 1923-1985 | United States. Army. Armored Division, 4th. | World War, 1939-1945—Campaigns—Western Front. | World War, 1939-1945—Personal narratives, American. | United States. Army. Armored Infantry Battalion, 53rd. Company B. | Soldiers—United States—Biography.
Classification: LCC D769.3053 4th .P67 2024 | DDC 940.541273092 [B]—dc23/eng/20240816
LC record available at https://lccn.loc.gov/2024032548

BRITISH LIBRARY CATALOGUING DATA ARE AVAILABLE

ISBN (print) 978-1-4766-9570-9
ISBN (ebook) 978-1-4766-5373-0

© 2024 Colleen C. Porter. All rights reserved

No part of this book may be reproduced or transmitted in any form or by any means, electronic or mechanical, including photocopying or recording, or by any information storage and retrieval system, without permission in writing from the publisher.

Front cover images: : Private Paul Porter. This photograph appeared on a Fourth Armored Division Christmas card for the 1943 holiday (Colleen C. Porter family collection). *Background*: men of the 53rd Armored Infantry Battalion near Baerendorf, France, on November 25, 1944 (U.S. Army photograph).

Printed in the United States of America

*McFarland & Company, Inc., Publishers
Box 611, Jefferson, North Carolina 28640
www.mcfarlandpub.com*

This work is dedicated
to the soldiers of Company B
of the 53rd Armored Infantry Battalion,
Fourth Armored Division,
who along with my father, endured hardships
that no man deserves.
They have my utmost admiration,
respect, and gratitude.

Table of Contents

Acknowledgments — ix
Preface by Colleen C. Porter — 1
Preface by Don M. Fox — 4
Introduction — 11

Chapter 1—Welcome to Normandy — 25
Chapter 2—Death of a Lieutenant — 32
Chapter 3—Fighting Two Wars — 41
Chapter 4—Leaving the Hedgerows Behind — 49
Chapter 5—Don't Mess with a Dragon — 61
Chapter 6—Wine, Women and Troyes — 72
Chapter 7—God Takes Care of Drunks and Fools — 82
Chapter 8—The Mysteries of War — 92
Chapter 9—A New Buck Sergeant — 105
Chapter 10—Another Town to Clear — 114
Chapter 11—Give Me Liberty or Give Me Death — 131
Chapter 12—A Godforsaken Village — 139

Epilogue — 161
Chapter Notes — 175
Bibliography — 191
Index — 193

Acknowledgments

To the best of my knowledge, my father wrote this memoir on his own. It was a one-man show, consistent with the independence he displayed throughout his life. Getting his book to the finish line required the effort of many more people. I think my father and mother would be proud of what we've accomplished.

I'll start by thanking my brother, also named Paul. After Dad passed away, Paul had possession of the manuscript. While he didn't pick up on my father's attempts to have the work published, thankfully he held on to it and, before his own death, passed the manuscript to me. Had my brother not done so, Sergeant Porter's words would have been lost for all time.

The first person I enlisted to help with the manuscript was Ted Baldwin. I'll always remember his words of advice: "Don't let anyone tell you this is ordinary and that it's been done before." Ted did a significant amount of work putting my father's original manuscript into a digital format; it was not an easy task due to the age and weathering of the pages. Ted did a magnificent job.

I later shared Dad's work with retired Colonel Michael Leonard and his wife Lindy. Colonel Leonard urged me to move forward with the project, telling me that my Dad was the kind of man you want 100 more of next to you when you are in a fight. Given Colonel Leonard's decorated military experience and his status as a published author, I was highly motivated by his feedback. I am very thankful for the support and encouragement that he and Lindy provided.

My cousin Charlotte Mince Bourgeois converted the work into a Word document and suggested some minor edits. Thank you, Charlotte!

Acknowledgments

I also enlisted Michael Morrison for an additional review of the work. I'd like to thank him for his suggestions and encouragement.

Our family is very fortunate to have retained photographs of my mother and father dating back to the 1940s. Christopher Mathews did a superb job of digitizing and restoring the family photos used in the book. I am grateful for his effort.

World War II Armor is an organization committed to educating the public on the U.S. armor tactics, training, vehicles, and personnel of World War II. They maintain an impressive collection of fully operational armored vehicles and weapons which they display and put into action at public events. Their head of training and plans is Erik Albertson, and he and his team invited us to take photographs of the type of equipment used by my father while in combat. To learn more about their mission, I encourage you to visit WW2armor.org.

Don Fox is the author of the two-volume history of the Fourth Armored Division, *Patton's Vanguard* and *Final Battles of Patton's Vanguard*. When I first reached out to Don, it was to connect him with Colonel Leonard. To my surprise, he was already aware of my father's award of the Distinguished Service Cross. He even mentions it in *Patton's Vanguard*. Don became involved in the project in a way that I never imagined when I reached out to him. He fact checked the manuscript based upon his intimate knowledge of the Fourth Armored and vouched for its authenticity. He graciously wrote the introduction and epilogue to the present work. Finally, he prepared the endnotes that help make this a scholarly work as much as it is a memoir.

Don also helped me truly understand how hard my father's life had been before, during, and after World War II. Until then, I never really grasped the toll that the war had taken on him. This has been a hard journey for me and a very emotional one. Don, I thank you on behalf of my dad for making this dream—*his* dream—come true.

Mom and Dad, thank you for bringing me into this wonderful world. Dad, you told me to never give up on my singing, and I followed your advice. I wrote a tribute called *The Best of the USA* dedicated to you and all our great veterans:

Acknowledgments

My father is a veteran who fought in WW 2.
Over there in France and in Germany too.
He fought in rain sleet and snow and in weather 20 below.
He was highly decorated and in victory celebrated.
As the guns and bombs were blazing his courage was amazing
   today in America the bells of freedom ring.
To my father and all American veterans I sing.
To the American veterans I say
thank you for all the freedom that's mine today.
You fought the wars so I could be free
you'll go down in history as the best
the best of the USA

Dad, you are my song. Till we meet again.—Colleen C. Porter

Preface

by Colleen C. Porter

Paul S. Porter, my father, was a hero.

Yes, daughters often feel that way about their fathers, but in Paul Porter's case, it is not trite, or a matter of girlish enthusiasm. He had the papers to prove it; papers recording the presentation of medals and commendations for wartime service and heroism during World War II.

And now, we also have the record of his deeds in his own words. He was not just *any* hero. He was among the elite.

My father's combat experience began soon after his arrival in Normandy with the 53rd Armored Infantry Battalion and continued across France until he was within a few miles of the German border. He preserved his memories in a manuscript, which contains a level of detail that is rare among wartime memoirs. Many men that experienced what my father did, did not live to tell the tale. That he survived such harrowing experiences and had the ability to write in such rich, compelling detail, is a unique combination. We are fortunate that the manuscript survived and is seeing the light of day nearly 40 years after his death.

Like war itself, his account is bloody, sad, heart-breaking, and discouraging, but often counterbalanced by the less serious proclivities of youth. After all, he and his fellow soldiers were, by and large, boys and young men. Paul Porter certainly took youthful qualities with him when he crossed the Atlantic.

Like many heroes, Paul Porter also had flaws, or perhaps better said, weaknesses. He exhibited some of those behaviors during

Preface by Colleen C. Porter

his time in France. We know too little about his early life to judge his character prior to going into combat. As his daughter, I can testify to his weaknesses following the war. Having absorbed his manuscript, I now have a better understanding and empathy for the man he became.

Dad typed the manuscript himself. We have evidence that he was asked to submit the manuscript to an agent in 1967, but he never followed up on it.[1*] He lamented not doing so in a hand-written note composed on July 20, 1978, seven years before his death. His reflection must have inspired action. On October 28 of that year, he paid a $150 reading fee to a literary agent. What came of that, we don't know, other than the fact that it remained unpublished.

The weathered, typewritten pages remained in the family after my father passed. Paul, my only sibling, gave me the manuscript prior to his own death in 2022. It was my first opportunity to read it, and after doing so, I felt compelled to seek its publication. Paul S. Porter should not be my hero alone.

The editing in preparation for publication is limited. There is some minor editing for clarity, correction of spelling for some towns and rivers, and a few instances where he misidentified a combat unit or was mistaken on a date; we corrected those in the narrative. Our primary mission was to preserve the authenticity of his account. It is *his* voice, expressing the things that only *his* senses could perceive: the sights, smells, sounds, and physical pain of combat.

My father was critical of several of the men he served with; he judged some of them harshly. We are in no position to second-guess his assessment of their character or courage. I hope that, should descendants of any of those men take offense at Paul's characterizations, they will understand our desire to preserve the integrity of the memoir. I am certain that my father would readily acknowledge his *own* weaknesses; especially those that emerged in the wake of his combat experience. I also suspect that he would never begrudge anyone calling him out. Instead, he would respect them for their candor.

Paul Porter was a hero, but he wasn't the only one. He served

---

*See Notes section at the back of the book, chapter-by-chapter.

Preface by Colleen C. Porter

among a company of heroes. I respect and admire them all and I am thankful for their service and sacrifice. This is also *their* story ... the story of Company B of the 53rd Armored Infantry Battalion. To paraphrase the great leader of the Fourth Armored Division, Major General John Shirley Wood, let us never forget their deeds.[2]

Preface

by Don M. Fox

Paul S. Porter served with great distinction during the Second World War. His highest accolade was the Distinguished Service Cross (DSC), which ranks second only to the Medal of Honor as the most prestigious award a member of the United States Army can receive.

The action that resulted in his DSC is well documented. But like so many veterans, little was known about the balance of his wartime experience. Unlike the millions of others who served, in Paul's case, this has been remedied, thanks to the effort of his daughter, Colleen Porter, who resurrected Paul's previously unpublished wartime memoir.

When I read the manuscript, I was awed by the gritty detail and candor that Sergeant Porter committed to paper. I have read numerous memoirs and interviewed many World War II veterans. None of them articulated their experience in as riveting and compelling a fashion as Porter. He writes in a captivating style; his voice is uniquely his own. His words and emotions sprint across the pages.

Porter's writing is *so* compelling that one might question its authenticity. It is unfortunate, but perhaps simply a matter of human nature, that some memoirs are blemished by embellishment, sensationalism, hyperbole, and faulty memories. Some, when composed at a time further removed from events, suffer from forms of revisionism.

As the author of the two-volume history of the United States Army Fourth Armored Division, I was well positioned to scrutinize

Preface by Don M. Fox

the manuscript for its alignment with the historical record. One must dig deep into the after-action reports and other historical documents to corroborate elements of Sergeant Porter's narrative. At nearly every turn, his recollections were in sync with the history of Company B of the 53rd Armored Infantry Battalion, Fourth Armored Division, the unit in which he served.[1*]

I was especially eager to research and validate the names of the officers and enlisted men Porter mentioned in his manuscript. One of the most compelling aspects of Paul's writing is that, when it comes to those he served with, he called it the way he saw it, whether it cast an unfavorable light or not. While I could not collect information on all of them, many of the names were verified. I found no evidence of fictionalized characters.

Another aspect of Paul's manuscript that is unlike many other World War II memoirs is that it begins and ends with his combat experience. He sheds little light on his life prior to arriving in Normandy on July 14, 1944, nor of what happened after he was evacuated from the battlefield on December 4 of that same year. Fortunately, his daughter Colleen helped develop a broader picture of who Paul Porter was; a man too modest to mention his DSC. During our work on the book, her insights, gleaned from her personal experience and her years of interaction with other family members, were invaluable for painting a picture of Paul's life before and after the war.

Paul's narrow focus on his combat experience may leave a gap for some readers. Those who are well-equipped with knowledge of World War II military history may be able to place his account into context. Laypersons, however, will be at a disadvantage. I will attempt to close that gap.

Let's start by recognizing Sergeant Porter's role from a big-picture perspective. During World War II, approximately 16 million people served in the military of the United States of America. Most of those men and women were in roles that, while essential for achieving victory, didn't bring them face-to-face with the enemy. They never heard the whine of a bullet much less stare down

---
*See Notes section, separate for each chapter.

the barrel of a gun. They never felt the crushing concussion of an exploding artillery shell, the indiscriminate harbinger of dismemberment or death. They never experienced the split-second moment of dread that accompanied the realization that a landmine had been triggered. These things, and so many other dangers and hardships, were reserved for those who, by choice or assignment, were at the tip of the spear. Sergeant Porter did not serve among the privileged class. He served at the opposite end of the spectrum. He was a combat soldier, an infantryman, through and through.

A variety of roles introduced men to combat, but none carried the risk of death that came with being an infantryman. An examination of the casualties from within his own Fourth Armored Division reflects the danger he faced. For example, the 22nd Armored Field Artillery Battalion suffered 24 men killed in action (KIA) during the 10 months the division served in combat.[2] The 24th Armored Engineer Battalion, working closer to the front lines than the artillery, suffered 44 KIA. The 8th Tank Battalion, its tanks facing the direct fire of some of the most powerful weapons of the era, suffered 106 KIA. In stark contrast, the 53d Armored Infantry Battalion, which at full strength was comprised of 1001 men, had *286 men killed in action*; just shy of 19 percent of the 1,519 KIA for the total division.[3] With little but their wool uniform separating them from the tip of a bullet or a jagged, searing-hot piece of shrapnel, they were the most vulnerable of all warriors on the battlefield.

Within the ranks of an armored infantry battalion, not all roles were equal. All carried their fair share of danger, to be sure, but the heaviest burdens were shouldered by the men who served within the battalion's three rifle companies, labelled with no fanfare as A, B, and C. The rifle company was in turn comprised of a company headquarters (two officers and 48 enlisted men), an antitank platoon (one officer and 32 enlisted men equipped with three towed 57 mm antitank guns), and three rifle platoons, each of which was comprised of one officer and 55 enlisted men.[4]

The rifle platoon was where the action was the hottest. A lieutenant would normally be in command of the unit. The platoon was comprised of three rifle squads, a 60 mm mortar squad, and

Preface by Don M. Fox

a light machine gun squad. The standard weapon for the infantryman was the venerable M1 Garand rifle. Some members of the company (including the officers) were armed with the lighter M1 carbine. Heavier firepower in the form of an M2 .50 caliber machine gun was mounted on each of the M3A1 half-tracks used to transport the company. The half-track was, in many respects, the infantryman's second home during their journey across Europe.

Sergeant Porter served as a member of the light machine gun squad in the third platoon of Company B, 53rd Armored Infantry Battalion. His view of the war comes to us through the prism of his company. We learn much about the tactics upon which the infantryman relied, not because Porter is trying to school us, but because he writes in such riveting detail about his experience on the battlefield.

What Porter's account *doesn't* communicate is the pivotal role the Fourth Armored Division played during the war. The division was arguably the best division in the United States Army. The Fourth served as the vanguard of Patton's Third Army as it burst through the German defenses near Avranches on the heels of Operation Cobra. Commanded by Major General John Shirley Wood,[5] the division dashed magnificently across the neck of the Brittany Peninsula and soon turned east into the interior of France. Wood's men

A gunner and ammunition handler work a tripod-mounted .30 caliber light machine gun M1919A4 (U.S. Army photograph).

fought brilliant battles at Orleans and Troyes and sped relentlessly east toward Germany until gasoline shortages brought their tanks and half-tracks to a halt. Once back in supply, the Fourth plunged across the Moselle River and soon found itself engaged in the greatest tank-versus-tank battle of the 1944–45 campaign in Western Europe. After a respite from mid–October to early November, the division entered an intense period of combat and slugged its way closer to the German border.

The shooting war ended on December 4 for Sgt. Porter. For the rest of the Fourth Armored, another five months of combat remained. The Battle of the Bulge was yet to come, followed by a brilliant drive into Germany that brought the division to the Rhine River on March 8. By the time the war ended, they had advanced into Czechoslovakia.

The accomplishments of the division were recognized most notably when the Fourth Armored became one of only two divisions to receive the Presidential Distinguished Unit Citation (the other being the 101st Airborne Division). There were 16 American armored divisions activated during the war, and the Fourth stood out among them. Members of the division earned 34 Distinguished Service Crosses (Sgt. Porter being among them), well above the 21 DSCs earned by members of the Second Armored Division (the armored division with the next highest total).[6]

During the 144 days in France before his evacuation from the battlefield, Sgt. Porter experienced time away from the front line. His proclivities and foibles on those occasions (though I doubt he would describe them that way) are not as easily verified as are his acts of heroism. We are left to take him at his word in respect to those exploits, with the caveat that his accuracy in describing other events leaves us no reason to doubt him. Still, it will be up to the reader to make their own decision on that count.

On the one hand, it is a shame that Sgt. Porter's story was not published sooner. I am quite confident that had it made its way into print decades ago, it would have stood the test of time and spent the following years as one of the best combat memoirs ever published for an American soldier. Yes, it would have even rivaled *Company*

Commander by the late Charles B. MacDonald, which was published in 1947 and has stood for all these years as a classic battlefield memoir.

On the other hand, even though it is 80 years after Porter's combat experience, it is not too late for his story to set a new standard. Perhaps there are other undiscovered manuscripts that will one day come into print and rival Porter's account. I wouldn't bet on it though.

Introduction

Little in life came easy for Paul Samuel Porter. When he and his fraternal twin brother Silas entered the world on September 26, 1923, they were the eighth and ninth children of William Monroe Garfield Porter and his wife Nora Mae. Wealth can mitigate the type of hardships that Paul faced between his birth and being drafted into the U.S. Army in 1943, but the Porters were on the opposite end of the financial spectrum, trying to make ends meet on farmland near the tiny town of Brushy, Oklahoma.

Perhaps it was a blessing to have twin boys born into a farmer's family. Strong hands and backs were valued, and sons were a long time coming for William and Nora Mae. Ethel, the couple's first child born in 1909, was followed by four consecutive girls, each arriving two years after the other. The Porters' first boy, William Monroe, was born in 1919, two years after the birth of his sister Doris Dean. William was followed by John, yet again, two years later. And then finally, after another two years, came Paul and Silas.[1]

William Porter and Nora Mae McKinney had married in 1908, right there in Brushy.[2] It is where they met and where they remained throughout their marriage. Brushy was Nora Mae's hometown, but it was not William's. Paris, Texas, which is about 140 miles south of Brushy, was his place of birth in 1886.

A constant for William was living the life of a farmer. As far as we know, it was his only occupation before he met Nora Mae, and the one he maintained throughout their marriage.[3] Nora Mae was six years his junior and only 16 years old when they married. Modest means throughout their marriage didn't deter the couple from raising a large family.[4]

Introduction

The Porter brothers; from left: John, William, Silas, and Paul (Colleen C. Porter family collection).

If giving birth to William's namesake in 1919 was a source of joy for the Porters, it was an emotion more than offset by the loss of their daughter Bessie when she was just a few weeks shy of turning six. Paul, of course, wasn't alive yet, and was spared the scar of losing a sister; he never knew her, other than what his parents and oldest siblings might have told him in later years. As the family mourned Bessie's death, what none of the Porters knew was that this was just the first of many tragedies they would endure during the years ahead. Paul and Silas, as the youngest, were perhaps the most vulnerable ... and they were tested all too soon. In 1929, Paul's mother passed away. Nora Mae was only 39 years old. She left behind her husband and eight children ranging in age from 6 to 20.

The weight on the shoulders of Paul's father must have been immense, especially given the timing relative to world events. The Great Depression began that same year. Two years later, extreme

Introduction

drought and high winds—what came to be known as the Dust Bowl—turned the agricultural landscape of the Southern Plains into a disaster area. Oklahoma was especially hard hit. People fled west in droves in pursuit of better conditions and jobs. Several members of the Porter family joined the exodus.

By 1935, 12-year-old Paul was living in San Joaquin County, California. We don't know whose custody he was in; his father was in Tulsa, Oklahoma, as was his sister Doris Dean. Though his family was splintered, Paul completed elementary school. His formal education ended after his first year of high school.

The picture becomes a little clearer in 1937. We know that Doris married Bosman C. Kent, a dairyman, on September 2 of that year in the town of Florence, Arizona. The Kents had their first-born child, Jerry, on May 2, 1939. We also know from the 1940 Census that by then, 17-year-old Paul was living with the Kents in the town of Blythe, California, an agricultural community on the California–Arizona border 140 miles west of Phoenix.

Paul Porter and his sister Doris. This photograph predates Paul's entry into the U.S. Army (Colleen C. Porter family collection).

Introduction

Paul wasn't the only Porter living under the Kents' roof. His father had remarried, and the couple joined the Kents. The household income was low. William, who left farming to become a preacher, earned $500 a year.[5] His new wife Virgie Mae, a native of Oklahoma, worked as a laundress, earning half of what her husband produced. Paul, though having abandoned school and being able-bodied, apparently didn't work in either 1939 or 1940.[6]

We don't know the exact timing, but other members of the Porter family headed west as well. Ella Mae, second oldest among Paul's siblings, had moved to Riverside, California, by 1940. William, the oldest son, landed in California as well and while there was drafted into the U.S. Army; he was the first of the four Porter sons to serve. During the month of November 1941, he was one of 52 men from the Santa Maria area headed for induction. Most of the men were processed locally, but ten of them were sent to other districts. William's destination was Woodhaven, New York, the farthest of the lot.[7]

The second oldest son, John B., was unemployed and living in Santa Maria when he registered for the draft on Valentine's Day of 1942. Though living far from his sister Doris, he named her the person who would always know his address.[8] He ended up serving in the U.S. Army. Paul's fraternal twin, Silas, joined the Merchant Marines.

The reunion between Paul and his father didn't last long. In 1942, Paul's father and stepmother headed north to a new home not far north of Oakland, where he served as a preacher employed by the Free Holiness Church based in Ramona, Oklahoma, a small town 25 miles north of Tulsa.[9] William Porter's stay in the Oakland area appears short, as he returned to Oklahoma sometime during 1943.

Paul did not follow his father back to Oklahoma. He remained in California and moved north to the Fresno area along with the Kent family.

On June 30, 1942, nine months after his 18th birthday, Paul registered for the draft. He had grown into a strong young man, especially for those times: five-feet eleven-inches and a muscular 181 pounds. He claimed to be unemployed.[10]

When Paul registered, he, like his brother John, listed their sister Doris as his closest contact. At that time, she lived in Hanford,

Introduction

which is 25 miles south of Fresno. Paul submitted his address as being in Firebaugh, 35 miles west-northwest of Fresno.

Unlike many of his generation, Paul was in no hurry to join the war effort. However, the draft caught up to him (despite his later claims of trying to outrun it) and he was inducted into the Army on May 14, 1943. He left his home, which by then had shifted to Richmond, California, and headed to New Orleans for his induction. When Uncle Sam finally grabbed Paul by the collar, the Porter family was all in.

Before Paul turned his body and mind over to the Army, it appears that he gave his heart to Joyce Anna Martin, a beautiful, 16-year-old native of Louisiana. We know little of how they met during whatever time he had in New Orleans, but it was enough to ignite a love interest.[11]

After Paul's induction, we know more about the path he followed, but little about his personal experience as he navigated

Left: Joyce Anna Martin (Colleen C. Porter family collection). *Right:* Private Paul Porter. Photograph taken prior to the Fourth Armored Division's departure for England. Location and date of the photograph is unknown (Colleen C. Porter family collection).

Introduction

training. His first stop was Fort Knox, Kentucky, home of the fledgling Armor School. A common denominator for men assigned to armored divisions was mechanical aptitude; Paul's experience on farms may have been an attribute that led to his eventual assignment to the Fourth Armored Division.

By the time Paul caught up with the Fourth Armored, they were training at Camp Bowie, Texas. The division had already completed its initial training at Pine Camp in upstate New York, followed by extensive training at the California Desert Training Center and Camp Ibis.[12]

On September 10, 1943, the Fourth Armored Division went through a reorganization that led to the formation of three armored infantry battalions: the 10th, 51st, and 53rd. Lieutenant Colonel George L. Jaques commanded the 53rd, the battalion to which Paul Porter was assigned.[13] On the day the battalion was established, the total strength was 31 officers, three warrant officers, and 892 enlisted men.[14]

Paul was assigned to Company B as a member of the light machine gun squad. The squad consisted of a staff sergeant who served as the squad leader, an assistant squad leader (normally a sergeant), a half-track driver, two machine gunners, two ammunition handlers, and

Private Paul Porter. The photograph was taken in 1943 during Porter's time at Camp Bowie, Texas, and sent to his future wife, Joyce (Colleen C. Porter family collection).

16

Introduction

five riflemen. The 12-man squad fit snuggly in the M3A1 half-track. There were three machine guns: a powerful .50 caliber Browning M2 mounted on a ring above the cab of the vehicle, and two .30 caliber Browning M1919A4 light machine guns mounted one on each side of the half-track.[15] All of the machine guns could be detached from their mounts and placed on tripods in the field. The light machine guns were much easier to move than the massive M2. Indeed, if the gunner was strong enough, the .30 caliber could be fired from the hip. Paul's role was a gunner for one of the light machine guns.

Road marches, range firing, and the "usual camp duties" dominated the agenda at Camp Bowie. Every so often, there were activities that broke the monotony. On September 28, for example, Company B participated in swimming instruction at Brownwood Lake.

Then Major George L. Jaques in a picture that appeared in the *Historical and Pictorial Review Fourth Armored Division–51st Armored Infantry Regiment*. Popularly known as the "Pine Camp books," the multi-volume publication was produced in 1942 and captured the personnel of the division at that time. Jaques then served in the dual roles of S-2 and S-3 and would later ascend to command the 53rd Armored Infantry Battalion (U.S. Army photograph).

During mid–October, a more ambitious, six-day exercise helped prepare the battalion for attacks against fortified positions. Demonstrations were conducted on the use of satchel and pole charges. On the final day of the exercise, the 53rd AIB attacked the fortifications in concert with the 35th Tank Battalion, 66th Armored Field

Introduction

Artillery Battalion, and Company B of the 24th Armored Engineer Battalion. It was the type of combined arms task force training that would pay dividends when the men entered combat.

On December 14, Company B departed Camp Bowie and boarded trains bound for Camp Myles Standish in Massachusetts. They arrived on December 17. Four days later they began preparing for their move to England.

Company B departed Camp Myles Standish by train at 0650 hours on December 29. It was a short trip, and the entire battalion embarked on the USAT Santa Paula at 0900 hours. At 1430 hours, they set sail from Boston Harbor.[16] After 10 days at sea, they docked at Swansea, Wales. The battalion disembarked the night of January 10 and boarded a train for Devizes, a small town about 80 miles west of London. They arrived at their new home, Prince Maurice Barracks, at 0330 hours on January 11.

Private Paul Porter. This photograph appeared on a Fourth Armored Division Christmas card for the 1943 holiday (Colleen C. Porter family collection).

Throughout the balance of January, the battalion settled into their new environment. The entire Fourth Armored Division drew new equipment (they did not bring any with them from the United States; equipment was already staged there) and renewed their training.

There were several highlights during the weeks that followed. On February 2, the battalion area was visited by Lt. Gen. Patton, who followed his inspection with an address to all the officers. Field training was supplemented with classroom work,

Introduction

including a session on February 3 titled "What to Do in the Event of Capture."[17]

Forms of recreation crept into the battalion's schedule. On February 6, there was a "recreation convoy" to Bath, a slightly larger town 16 miles west of Devizes. On the night of February 9, Company B held a dance party in the town hall of Devizes. As the weather improved, competitive softball games were a favorite pastime. By the end of the month, the intensity of training increased, culminating in a significant combined-arms exercise that involved the reduction of a town.

March was more of the same, with at least one exception being the administration of vaccinations against smallpox and a "stimulating shot of Tetanus and Typhoid."[18] Several officers and enlisted men received specialized training on a variety of subjects. Paul Porter was not among them. The young private, at least as far as we can tell from the battalion records, flew under the radar.

During April, the men were exposed to an array of weapons to broaden their expertise. They learned more about the enemy by studying their uniforms and rank of insignia. They also learned about the operation of German weapons. Security tightened around

To become familiar with and learn the capabilities of German weapons, U.S. infantrymen fired them during training. The soldiers in the picture are manning a German M.G. 34 machine gun (U.S. Army photograph).

Introduction

the base, presumably due to the impending invasion of France; restricted movement was imposed on several occasions.

On April 21, Lt. Gen. Patton visited and spent the night in the battalion area. That same day, a recreational convoy took members of the battalion to Salisbury, 20 miles south of Devizes, where they saw a boxing exhibition by heavyweight champion of the world Staff Sergeant Joe Louis.

On April 26, the tactical exercise for the day was given a twist when Lt. Col. Jaques withdrew the normal staff officers from the exercise and placed other officers in charge, thus replicating what would happen if the battalion suffered serious losses at the higher levels of command (including the loss of Jaques). Captain Henry A. Crosby ... an officer who would figure prominently in Paul's future ... took command of the battalion for the exercise.

May 8 marked the start of another major exercise. That evening, the battalion traveled 13.8 miles to Westdown Range, located two miles east of Tilshead.[19] Once there, they started preparing for a demonstration that would be observed by Lt. Gen. Patton and their division commander, Major General John S. Wood. The Fourth Armored Division's three armored field artillery battalions and a platoon of medium tanks from the 37th Tank Battalion would also participate. The two generals, who were great friends from West Point, observed the rehearsals on May 9 as well as the demonstration conducted the following day. After the exercise, Lt. Gen. Patton spoke to the officers involved and "complimented them very highly on a job well done."[20]

Organized softball games remained popular. On May 13, Company B scored a 4–1 victory over the team from Division HQ. It must have been a matter of pride, as the outcome made its way into the battalion diary along with the comment that it "was the first defeat for Division HQ Team since arrival in ETO."

In early June, the battalion left for a new camp near Lydiard Millicent, 16 miles north of Devizes. The routines remained much the same, though a new twist was a lecture held on June 12 that focused on the "Control of Venereal Disease." Conspicuously absent from the unit diary for June was any mention of D-Day.

Introduction

On July 1, the men became aware that their turn at combat was drawing near. At 0930 hours, the entire battalion was assembled and then informed by Lt. Col. Jaques that they would soon be moving to the marshalling area.

The tempo slowed during the next few days. On July 5, all members of the battalion received a physical inspection by the battalion surgeon. The most exciting news for the week may have been Company B's extra-innings victory over the team from Headquarters Company.

American trucks disembark from a Landing Ship—Tank (LST) on one of the beaches of Normandy, France (U.S. Army photograph).

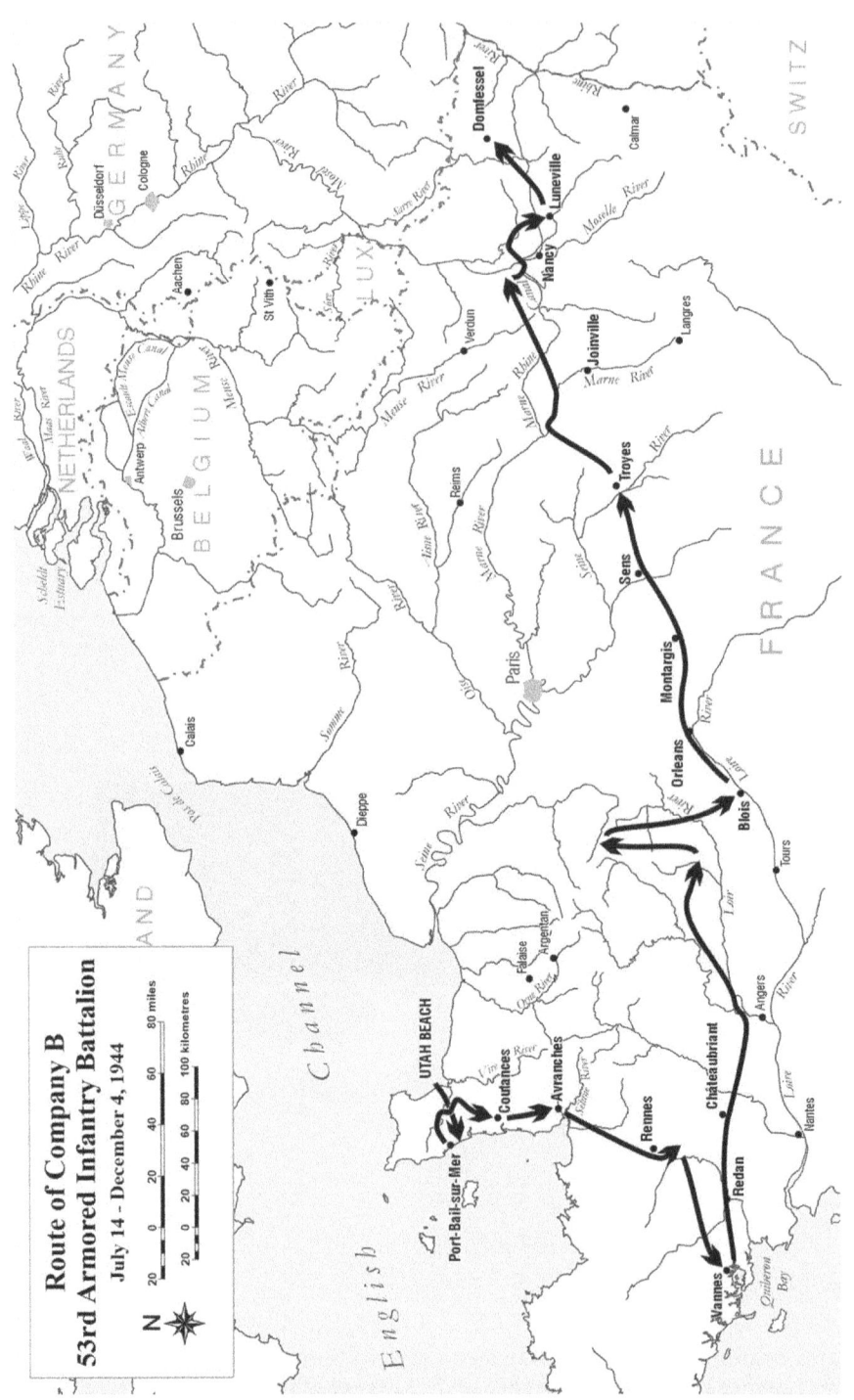

Introduction

On July 8, word arrived that the battalion would depart for the marshalling area at 0645 hours the following day. Things were about to get very real for Paul Porter and the other 1,000 men of the 53rd Armored Infantry Battalion.

While Paul digested the news of the impending move to the coast of Normandy, he was unaware of events that day on the other side of the Atlantic. In the town of Ramona, Oklahoma, Virgie Mae Porter gave birth to her first child and her husband's tenth. Patricia Mae Porter came into the world on July 8, 1944. Paul gained a stepsister but lost his stepmother: Virgie Mae did not survive childbirth. Yet another tragedy had befallen the Porter family. It was not the last.

Company B arrived in the marshalling area on July 9. They gassed their vehicles and prepared their equipment for loading onto the ship that would take them across the English Channel. Moving the division to Normandy was a massive undertaking. The 53rd AIB spent the next two days waiting for their turn to move to the port for embarkation. Company B finally left for Weymouth at 0105 hours on July 12. They boarded their LST (Landing Ship Tank) at 1600 hours and set sail at 0430 hours on July 13. Their LST arrived at Sugar Red Beach at 2000 hours and remained offshore the remainder of the night. Finally, at 1030 hours on July 14, the 1,001 men of the 53rd Armored Infantry Battalion disembarked from the ship and rolled 31 miles toward their assembly area beyond the shores of Normandy.

Few could have imagined what was in store during the weeks and months ahead. Many would not live to tell their story. Survivors often had little interest in sharing their experience; they would rather purge the sights, sounds, and smells of war from their minds; something that was impossible to do. There were some, however, who were compelled to tell their story, if not immediately upon their return from the war, then years later. One of those men was Sergeant Paul S. Porter. The words you are about to read are his. No one could have told it better.

Opposite: **The route followed by Paul Porter's Company B, 53rd Armored Infantry Battalion, during the campaign in France (© Petho Cartography, 2023).**

Chapter 1

Welcome to Normandy

Company B of the 53rd Armored Infantry Battalion, 4th Armored Division, landed in Normandy (Utah Beach) on the 14th day of July 1944, one month and eight days after D Day.[1]* As we moved our half-tracks through the countryside there in Normandy on that sultry day, we could see the evidence of much hard fighting that had taken place in the days prior to our landing. That first night, we bivouacked in an apple orchard. The half-tracks, which we called tracks, were spread out some fifty yards apart, and, at two or three in the morning, our company commander sent out a roving patrol to make sure that all tracks had a sentry posted.

This proved to be a very foolish action on the part of the company commander, but he was as green as a gourd, just as green as the men he had selected to make the patrol. One of the men selected wasn't too bright. He approached the half-track of one Jim Cardone, who stood silently in the darkness guarding the fast asleep men of his squarely dug-in squad.[2]

The sharp command of Jim's voice came out of the darkness like the crack of a .45. "Halt! Halt! Who goes there?"

Jim's voice, breaking through the stillness, alerted the latent fear that hid itself in the bosom of "The Preacher," which was the misnomer of the man who approached Jim's half-track. He turned quickly and began to run for the cover of the dark Normandy night. Thinking the man to be an encroaching enemy, Jim raised his rifle, and, in one quick motion, yanked the trigger.

The rifle had been instinctively pointed in the direction of the fleeing man, and the bullet struck him, felling him to the ground

---

*See Notes section at the back of the book, chapter-by-chapter.

The M3A1 half-track was the armored transport used by the armored infantry battalions. The pictured half-track is part of the collection maintained by the organization World War II Armor (photograph by Don M. Fox).

with a gaping wound in his hip. His name was the first to enter the company roster, receiving the distinguished asterisk, "Wounded in combat."

Jim Cardone himself earned the distinction of having fired the first shot on French terrain by Company B, 53rd Armored Infantry Battalion, 4th Armored Division. He was one of our own men.

Cardone's shot was the first of countless millions of rounds of ammunition that the men of the 53rd Battalion addressed to the care of those men who contributed to the delinquency of malingerers, who shirked their duties to mankind, and to those men who endeavor to usurp the authority of other men for their own personal aggrandizement.

Chapter 1. Welcome to Normandy

The Preacher had been a malingerer for as long as I had known him and had bucked for a section eight since he first entered the service.[3] He wouldn't take a bath if he had just crawled through a pig pen and there was water aplenty. He wouldn't shave properly. He wouldn't dress properly. He wouldn't keep his gear properly. As a matter of fact, that goddamn boy couldn't do anything right-properly. It was often said of him, "That boy just ain't right. He just ain't got no FUCKIN' COUTH."

It was a good thing that he was shot in the ass and got off the line, for had he continued with the company, he would more than likely have gotten some of us killed. He couldn't be depended upon when the noose began to get a little tight around the neck.

Jim did himself proud when he shot that boy in the rump instead of the head. He made a little opening to let in a little knowledge. The Preacher, on the other hand, would have been dangerous with just a little knowledge, for if we would march to war, we would do well to take more than just a little knowledge with us (Confucius).[4]

At daybreak on July 17, we mounted up and started moving toward the front, some fifteen miles away, where we were to relieve a company of the 4th Infantry Division.[5] We passed their artillery, which was silent at the moment, and proceeded through the deathlike stillness that hovered over the countryside, a hundred yards beyond their position, where the column stopped.

We sat in the half-tracks for the space of a minute or two, looking at the unfamiliar terrain that had been razed by the artillery of both armies. The silence screamed to us from out of the countryside, causing an awareness to creep over the men in the track; causing us to know that there was impending death in the land. The sharp report of the cannon, a hundred yards to our rear, broke the stillness with unexpected clamor. The men in the tracks, having been hypnotized by the utter silence that prevailed a moment before, flinched in startled amazement, as their senses were recalled from the grave of stillness back to the realm of fear and the awareness of life.

Our artillery was engaging its German counterpart, sending a barrage of high explosives over our heads in a sharp whistling dirge, denoting death. The column moved under the cover of the artillery barrage to a position 1500 yards behind the immediate front, where we dismounted, taking full field packs with extra socks, shorts, undershirts, blankets; extra parts for the machine guns, ammunition aplenty. Bazookas and extra bandoleers, thrown around our necks like Poncho Villa's bandits, and on, and on, and on. You name it. We had it.

As we passed a group of men from the 4th Infantry Division, who had been fighting in the hedgerows for more than a month while we were still in England, waiting to be shipped to Normandy, one of them started to heckle us. "You guys ain't going to no picnic, you know. What in hell's name are you guys carrying all that equipment for? The first time them Krauts hit you fellers, you'll skin'er down and get rid of all that bullshit you're carrying."

Why hell's bells! We didn't know what the hell he was talking about and just kept moving past them. Nobody said too much to them because *we* knew that *they* knew we were greenies, and we weren't going to give them the opportunity to find out just how green we were.

We moved on through the hedgerows and came to the positions we were to relieve. They had been fighting from the beachhead, which was something like fifteen or twenty miles to the rear, pushing the Krauts in front of them, giving up a hedgerow or two, and losing men in every action ... like the proverbial frog in a well, who jumps up two feet and slides back one until he is finally on level ground.[6]

But by no wild stretch of the imagination had these men reached level ground, for the positions that we relieved were located hard against the hedgerow country. We could see the men of the 4th Infantry Division who had given up their lives in attempts to gain the next hedgerow, lying still in death, their bodies swollen to gaseous balloon-like forms, fifty yards to our immediate front in no man's land.[7]

Some of their bodies had swollen in the heat of July and burst like balloons. Others had been blown apart by the opposing artillery, their remains sending off a stink that hovered over their bodies like a heavy fog, while the green flies danced in jubilant glee.

The men of the 4th Infantry Division moved out of their holes

Chapter 1. Welcome to Normandy

Infantrymen resting in their foxhole in Normandy (U.S. Army photograph).

and we of the 4th Armored Division moved in, bag and baggage. We sat there in our respective foxholes for the remainder of the day, not knowing what was held in store for us. Never having been fired upon by an enemy, who themselves were fighting for their very existence, we had no concept of the hostility of war when it is brought into your own front door and there creates havoc and confusion that cannot be reckoned with.

The S.S. troopers that opposed our positions had been ordered by no less an authority than Hitler to hold each foot of ground at all

A M7 self-propelled howitzer from Battery B of the 22nd Armored Field Artillery Battalion, Fourth Armored Division (U.S. Army photograph).

costs.[8] The remains of the men that lay in no man's land were sufficient evidence to the eyes of the beholder to erase any doubt from the mind that they were cognizant of the order from on high, and that they were further aware of the consequence of failure to carry out the order to a final state of fruition. These S.S. troopers were mean bastards at best, and now that the "Little Corporal" had interceded, they became veritable sonsabitches and fought like wolverines.[9]

Occasionally, a few rounds of artillery passed over our heads, evidently searching for the location of our batteries that had moved into the positions previously occupied by the artillery of the 4th Infantry Division. During that first day on the line and all through the night, we hung in close to our trenches, not daring to go beyond a few feet from them, as we were not at all sure of the exact location of the nearby enemy. They, however, gave us time for orientation, and didn't send any of their artillery into our frontal positions but focused all their attention to the rear of us.

As the shells whistled over our heads, we became accustomed to

Chapter 1. Welcome to Normandy

their different directions by the sounds emitted by the various caliber cannon, sending their projectiles on their mission of destruction. For the first few hours after our arrival and occupancy of the 4th Infantry Division's positions, we remained in our trenches. But when we became aware of the duel that was raging between the batteries of the opposing artillery and our own, we climbed out of our trenches and lounged around on the ground beside them. As the heavier artillery of the enemy engaged their services toward the destruction of our corps artillery, we became familiar with the trajectory and intent of purpose of the larger projectiles, for they gave off a whooshing sound much the same as would be audibly evinced by catapulting a ten-gallon keg of nails through the air at approximately two thousand feet per second. "That one is for Division. That one for the company commander. That's for Old Man George" (Patton), the voices could be heard saying, as the artillery shells sailed over our heads.

Although the men of Company B showed no visible disposition to fear as we approached the front and took over the positions of the 4th Infantry, there was caution exercised for the first several hours. After we became familiar with the various sounds of sporadic small arms and artillery fire that came to our area from along the line, and after we were oriented in our positions, knowing the approximate location of the S.S. troopers who opposed us, much of the caution and our unrelaxed attitude left us and we fell to joshing each other, making wisecracks about the artillery shells that whistled overhead. We still didn't know what the score was, and at about four o'clock in the morning, it began to dawn on us that we were in no position to be joshing or joking about the surrounding circumstances, for the second man to distinguish himself with the asterisk behind his name on the company roster passed my position in a crouched attitude, running toward the line of trenches to my immediate right.

Chapter 2

Death of a Lieutenant

I hadn't paid too much attention to the dark form as it passed my foxhole, for I recognized the outline of the familiar G.I. helmet. I merely thought the man under the helmet to be one of our own men who had been to the rear on some official business. In less than five minutes I noticed the dark form of a man, as it leaped over the hedgerow, some fifty feet to my front, and continued across the open field.

I could still distinguish the very familiar G.I. helmet and paid it no further attention. The dark form of the man, running in a crouched attitude, continued across the field until it had reached a position twenty feet from the hedgerow it seemed so intent upon crossing. A voice called out of the night in very rapid order, "Halt! Halt! Halt!" But the form continued to move in the direction of the hedgerow, without taking heed of the command to halt. The darkness of the night was lit by five or six-foot-long tongues of fire that belched out of the muzzle of the carbine held by the man who had issued the order to halt. The dark form threw both arms into the air, stood upright for a moment, then fell backward to the ground, like a falling tree, and lay very still.

All through the night I sat in the foxhole, with nothing more than my head being visible above the ground. My rifle lay in front of me, with the safety off, fully loaded and primed to fire. My sense of hearing became so keen as to pick up the sound of a falling leaf as it struck the ground ten feet away.

All through the night I sat there, my eyes straining to pick out of the darkness anything contrary to nature. Anything that moved, even though ever so imperceptibly, caused my eyes to focus in that direction. My senses were being honed to a keen point of perception.

Chapter 2. Death of a Lieutenant

I was aware of the change coming over me, causing me to have eyes in the back of my head, causing me to taste the awareness with a keener sense of taste. I could hear better, see better, and think faster in the darkness. I was suddenly aware of a freedom I had longed for since I was old enough to think for myself. In the G.I. vernacular, I was truly being prepared for a baptism of fire. Although it was too early for me to know the real meaning of freedom in its fullest sense, I was awakening to an awareness of the fact that I was coming into this freedom in its infancy. I was also aware that there would be a period of growth before I knew what it meant to be free in the strictest sense of the word.

In the early morning hours, when a haze of dim light began to be noticed, breaking through the heavens, I crawled out of my foxhole and walked approximately one hundred and fifty feet to the rear, crossing a hedgerow that separated our positions. I approached a big hole that could easily house a jeep, and found Sergeant Kelly[1] sitting there, crying.

Lieutenant Luxbacher,[2] the commander of the anti-tank platoon, sat on the lip of the hole while Dutch Wanosik,[3] a Polack from Dennison, Ohio, stood upright, just above them. "What's wrong, Kelly?" I asked, as I approached the hole. Kelly looked up at me with big tears running down his cheeks and answered, "Doss shot Lieutenant Duffy last night."[4]

He couldn't hold back the tears, the big Irishman with the soft heart, and didn't seem to care whether we saw him crying. He made no attempt to cover his anguish, and the groans of sorrow coming from his mouth shook his entire body. "Captain O'Brien[5] sent Lieutenant Luxbacher up here to get him," Kelly went on to say, as I stood there, looking down into the hole. I looked at Lieutenant Luxbacher, normally a dark-complexioned man but now yellowish white from the fear that was clawing at his guts, and asked him, "Why don't you go out there and get Lieutenant Duffy, Lieutenant?" He looked up at me and answered the query, "There's snipers out there, Porter."

"Ah, bullshit," I exclaimed, turning very quickly from the hole, walking across the open field to the spot where Lieutenant Duffy's body lay, staring with unseeing eyes into the empty Normandy sky.

Four or five of the shots that had issued from the muzzle of Doss's carbine had struck Duffy full in the face, punching small round holes the size of a pencil into the flesh where they entered. On closer inspection, I found that the back of his head had been torn away by the bone structure that had been knocked loose and pushed through it by the fleeing bullets.

I stooped over the lieutenant's body and grabbed him firmly around the waist, lifting him to my shoulder, with his head to my front. The blood squirted from the gaping wounds in his head and spilled down my trouser leg. I dropped his body back to the ground. I took the raincoat from the back of my web belt, and, wrapping it around his head, I tied the sleeves around his neck and hoisted him to my shoulder like a sack of cotton. I walked to the corner of the hedgerow, where Kelly and Luxbacher waited in the hole, and dropped Lieutenant Duffy's body before them.

"Here he is, Lieutenant," I said, looking at Luxbacher. He was so frightened that he wouldn't even look at the body of his fellow officer. I knew right then and there that my suspicions about Lieutenant Luxbacher a year before, when I had first joined the division in Texas, had been confirmed.[6] He was a no-good son-of-a bitch. Luxbacher was a fraternizing, two-faced first lieutenant, who played poker with the enlisted men at night, making wisecracks and joking during the course of the game, and gigged the hell out of them the next day for not having a collar buttoned on a fatigue jacket. He was a spit and polish bastard who would rawhide the hell out of a man, as long as he had the upper hand (bars). But when he got himself exposed to a dog fight, such as the one that had just taken place, he spilled his guts and tucked his tail between his legs and slinked off like a dog caught sucking eggs.

Doss, the mortar man, who shot Duffy, felt so bad about the incident that he remained in his foxhole all that day.[7] Although he did not allow himself to expose his emotions to the men around him, I knew he was tearing his guts out with remorse, for he was an extremely good-natured, sensitive man, and very quiet. He could not be blamed for what happened, but nonetheless, he did not cease to scourge his soul for having shot one of his own men. He sat in

Chapter 2. Death of a Lieutenant

his foxhole, which had been hard dug against a hedgerow, where the hanging branches of the trees, growing on the three-foot fence of earth at his back, hung down to form an umbrella-like cover around his position. He watched in silence as I carried Lieutenant Duffy's body across the field.

The lieutenant could not have been thinking properly. He knew that the men were green to the ways of war, and because of the inexperience of never having faced any enemy, were inclined to be a little trigger happy. He could have had no business so urgent that it could not have waited until morning, for any man in his right frame of mind would have known that there would be no sleeping on the part of any other man during his first night on the front lines. Sleep would not induce itself, nor vigilance relax, for the men could not be sure that the Krauts would not come spilling over the hedgerows at any moment.

The lieutenant, however, was under the impression that it was his duty to assure there was proper sentry and outpost standing picket beyond the line. For this reason, he had left the safety of his foxhole to the rear of my position and ran along the line, inspecting our positions. When Doss saw the dark form leap over the hedgerow a hundred feet in front of him, he had no way of knowing it was the lieutenant.

Now, Duffy's body lay on the ground at my feet, the back of his head torn away, his face a mass of coagulated blood; so young and so fair to look upon, yet so very still in the silence of death. Each time I looked at his limp form, lying there before me, my thoughts raced back through the months to remind me that this man had bugged me from the very first moment I laid eyes on him back at Camp Bowie, Texas, more than a year before.

At that time, I was 21 years old. Duffy could not have been more than 23. He was a second lieutenant then. Duffy had been brought up with a silver spoon in his mouth, while I had lived under practically every tree in the southwest. He had been exposed to books, while I was picking cotton, milking cows, irrigating alfalfa fields and pitching hay. He had studied theories, while I had applied them. He had never walked behind a plow, with a check line on his shoulder, nor had he the opportunity to look at the rear end of a team of horses as they strained against the collar, pushing the plow through the ground.

In all probability, he would have argued that a horse pulls the plow, when in reality, the collar is in front of the horse, and he *pushes* instead of pulls. The boy had no horse sense is what I am prone to say. Push or pull; what the hell difference does it make? Either way, I would have been satisfied. But Duffy could only see his side of the picture, and this was nothing more than a tangled mass of abstractions, thrown together in a web of utter confusion. I stood there, looking down at Duffy's body for the space of five minutes, waiting for Luxbacher to say something, but he never opened his mouth.

"Come on, Dutch. Let's rig up a stretcher for this man," I finally said, taking my eyes off Duffy and swinging them past the men in the hole to stare at the Polack, who was standing on the lip of the hole, just above Luxbacher. The two of us took our bayonets and hacked two saplings to the ground and trimmed their branches. We took a blanket of the same color gray the Kraut uniforms were molded in and tied it to the saplings to form a crude stretcher. The Krauts had moved out of the positions we now held, and in their haste, had left one of their blankets behind in a trench. Strange that a man, who had trained for more than three years, continually pouring over books that theorized the principles of war and the finer points of self-preservation, should be stretched out before me on a blanket that had covered the body of the enemy he had trained so long to destroy. He never even got to see them.

Luxbacher didn't have the guts to order the Polack and me to carry the stretcher back to the command post. When I saw he wasn't going to do a damned thing until he was pushed, I spoke to him, directing my dead stare in his direction in such a fashion as to leave no doubt in his mind that I thought he was a revolving son-of-a-bitch, because this is exactly what he was. He was a son-of-a-bitch any way you looked at him; sideways, backways, frontways, topside, bottomside; any side you looked at him, he has a son-of-a-bitch.

"We're ready Lieutenant!" But he didn't move. Finally, he mustered up the courage to look at me and stammered. "You and Dutch

Chapter 2. Death of a Lieutenant

carry Duffy, and I'll go on ahead and run interference for you." Goddamn his hide! He knew there were no Krauts between the command post and our position, but he just couldn't stand to be near Lieutenant Duffy's body. With this, he crawled out of the hole he had been in since he first got there an hour before and lit a shuck in the direction of the command post, a quarter of a mile to the rear.

Dutch and I picked up the stretcher and labored over the hedgerow, trying to keep in sight of Luxbacher, who had not waited to see what we were going to do, but leaped over the hedgerow in front of us, and trotted across the open field to disappear in the brush. The two of us laughed as Luxbacher disappeared into the brushy terrain, and Dutch remarked in mimicked tongue, "Why, that son-of-a-bitch is scared to death, Porter! Well, I'll be a goddamn son-of-a-bitch."

This was his favorite expression. He used it when puzzled, or when pleasantly surprised by the sight of someone close to him, whom he hadn't seen for some time.

We crossed two or three hedgerows and gained the small farm road that had been gnawed away by centuries of use and natural erosion until the bed of the road was no longer level with the surrounding terrain, but two or three feet lower than the fields on either side, and walked back in the direction of the rear. By this time, Lieutenant Luxbacher had completely disappeared. We were approximately half the distance from the front line to the command post when the Krauts decided to disturb the tranquility and laid a mean-ass barrage of artillery around us.

They would start by bringing their fire down on the command post, which was only two hundred yards further in the direction of the rear, then bring it slowly unto themselves until it was on a lateral with the trenches where no man's land began. Then they would traverse their fire, raking the entire front.

Dutch and I placed Duffy's body on the ground and hugged the side of the embankment that happened to be nearest the exploding shells. The roadbed afforded no mean protection, and we lay there for ten minutes or so before the Krauts decided we had been thoroughly baptized and lifted their barrage. During the baptism, we said nothing. When the fire was lifted, we walked back to the middle of the

A sunken road in Normandy occupied by American troops. The nature of the terrain in the region favored the German defenders (U.S. Army photograph).

road, lifted the stretcher, and continued in the direction of the command post, neither of us saying a word.

The bullshit had a way of disappearing very quickly when something of a more important nature was brought to bear. There was fear clutching at our guts as we waited with such uncertainty, and a period of quiet thanksgiving when the uncertainty had been dismissed from our minds. We approached the farmhouse, where Captain O'Brien had set up housekeeping, and from the yard we could find no movement whatsoever. The trees had taken a hell of a drubbing and stood silently; their boughs stripped of the summer leaves that hid their nakedness before the men of war came to destroy their beauty.

Dutch, carrying the front of the litter, stopped several feet in front of the farmhouse and called to the men inside. "Hey, Captain. What do you want us to do with Lieutenant Duffy's body?" The front door opened, and Lieutenant Luxbacher looked out at us. "Bring him around to the side of the shed, Dutch." As we carried the stretcher around to the side of the shed, I wondered what that bastard was

Chapter 2. Death of a Lieutenant

From left to right, the M1 Carbine, M1 Garand Rifle, and the Browning Automatic Rifle (commonly referred to as the BAR). Porter valued the lighter weight of the M1 Carbine (photograph by Don M. Fox).

doing in the farmhouse. It served the son-of-a-bitch right. If he hadn't been in such a hurry to get away from Lieutenant Duffy's body, he wouldn't have been caught in that great concentration of fire.

The Krauts knew the Old Man had his command post set up in the farmhouse and had taken the range coordinates with them when they hauled freight. The condition of the surrounding buildings was sufficient evidence that they had the zero on the location, for the artillery shells had literally torn the hell out of them.

As I looked at Lieutenant Duffy's personal effects, I couldn't help but throw my rifle over the fence and take his carbine, which lay at his side on the stretcher. I knelt at his side and loosened the web belt that was strapped around his waist. His trench knife, fitted with an attachment device that fastened to the muzzle of the carbine to turn the weapon into a bayonet, was attached to the web belt. I unhooked the belt at my waist and strapped the contraband equipment into position and walked to the shed.[8] There were three apple cider barrels of a thousand-gallon capacity, and I had myself a snort. We went back to the front and lounged around for the remainder of the day, listening to the sounds of sporadic small arms fire that occasionally disturbed the stillness of the countryside.

When darkness fell, we turned our minds to the long night before us and crawled back in our respective holes like so many groundhogs. The night passed uneventfully, save for a few occasional rounds of artillery fire going over our heads in the direction of the rear, and the answers from our batteries.

Chapter 3

Fighting Two Wars

The second day was spent much like the first. Everyone was sitting outside their trenches, chewing the fat and talking about Doss and Lieutenant Duffy. At about three in the afternoon, we ran out of water and the Polack and I volunteered to fill the canteens of the men in our squad, if for no other reason than to break the monotony and to get away from our holes for a while. We gathered the canteens and started toward the rear, where we fully intended to fill them with apple cider instead of the expected water. But after having traveled only a short distance down the same road we had carried Lieutenant Duffy, the Kraut artillery broke over our heads like a gaggle of geese in flight formation to sit down noisily in the command post.

Them goddamn Krauts sure got a hard on for the Old Man, I thought, as the whistling torpedoes sailed overhead. Looks to me like the Old Man would get the hell out of that house if it made the Heineys so goddamn mad by him just being there, I thought.

A full five minutes had gone by and still the artillery continued to whistle through the air. When they lifted the artillery they had concentrated on the command post, we continued down the sunken road and eventually came out into the yard at the side of the main house. "Son-of-a-bitch," I exclaimed, looking at the beating the area had taken. Further investigation of the devastated area revealed two men lying under a tree in front of the farmhouse.

We were able to identify them as Pfc. Konsicky and one we all called Pop. They were very dead. Pop had a hole in his forehead the size of a silver dollar and Konsicky held his guts in his hand. Very dead men, both of them.[1] They had been attached to the kitchen and evidently had been bringing Captain O'Brien some hot chow, when they were caught in a hail of shrapnel, which ended the captain's hot chow line, at least for the moment.

Of course, Konsicky had held a gun on me back in Texas, while I dug Captain O'Brien a hole in the ground that measured six by six by six. So, I didn't get too stirred up when I saw him lying there under the tree, with his guts in his hands. Pop was a very quiet man of 42, who had seen better days back on the farm. He could probably have been discharged had he had the gumption or the inclination to withdraw his services. But, alas, he had not.

We filled our canteens with cider instead of water and returned to our positions. A very short time after our return, the Krauts hit us with a blanket of 88s and mortar fire, which lasted 25 to 30 minutes. The mortar shells were coming down so rapidly, and so many of them were duds, it looked as though some crazy games were being played, with sticks literally walking across the ground.

The field seemed alive with explosions that ripped the air and shrapnel that tore through the trees, ripping them into eerie forms. I was scared but held my position, with my head and shoulders above the ground, my carbine stretched before me, waiting for the attack I was sure would

Private Paul Porter (left) with a fellow soldier (unknown) during training. The photograph was likely taken at Camp Bowie, Texas (Colleen C. Porter family collection).

Chapter 3. Fighting Two Wars

come. A mortar shell landed about ten feet from my position and cat walked across the carbine in my hands, coming to a stop at the side of a man named Kovacs, who was feeding a 60-millimeter mortar tube and returning death in kind to the Kraut position, just beyond the hedgerow in front of the field we were defending.[2]

He looked at the shell that had come to rest at his side, and, without so much as a thought, he grabbed his mortar tube, and leaping to his feet, he literally jumped a hedgerow four feet high and disappeared through the brush. The barrage stopped for the space of three minutes, and then the Krauts came across the field, with small arms and artillery fire cracking through the stillness like hailstones on a tin roof.

An infantryman prepares to fire an M2 60mm mortar (U.S. Army photograph).

Captain O'Brien sent an order to the front that we were to lay down our arms and surrender to the Krauts. Most of the men obeyed his command.

I told the Polack to let them go on ahead. We would lag behind to see what was going to happen. Most of the men ran past our position in the direction of the command post. Dutch and I remained where we were. After all of them had disappeared, we crawled out of our hole and walked very slowly in the direction they had taken.

We reached a very narrow field road, walled on either side by a growth of brush and small saplings. At one end of the road, a Kraut had set up a machine gun and was very busily firing on anyone daring to cross the road. I told Dutch to hang back and wait a few minutes. When the Kraut had relaxed for just one second, I took three running steps and threw myself across the narrow road into a briar patch. Dutch did the same. I don't remember feeling even one briar stinging me; I was very much preoccupied with the business end of a machine gun and had no time for such small wounds.

As we approached the command post, we could see that most of the men had taken up a position of surrender in a field, some 50 to 60 feet from the farmhouse. Dutch and I remained in the sunken road and crawled under a tree, which had been cut down by an artillery shell and was now lying across the road, forming a bridge-like affair three feet high, and affording protection from a burst directly overhead.

Captain O'Brien had ordered the German-speaking Sergeant Wuestenhagen to tie a piece of white cloth to a stick and crawl up on the hedgerow to wave the flag of surrender. He was calling out to them in Kraut, *"Kameraden, kameraden,* we surrender!"[3] The Germans, however, wanted no part of this action, for each time he crawled on the hedgerow, they'd open fire on him with a machine gun and he'd fall off that hedgerow like a poled hog.

They continued the machine gun fire for some time and then opened with their artillery which landed in the field where the men lay waiting to surrender. I remember seeing a sergeant from the anti-tank platoon, lying on his belly in the field, when an artillery shell hit a few feet from him. The shrapnel cut his belly completely out and he lay very still. I remember this man so well because he played a guitar. A man of music and peace was now very dead in a field of Normandy because of the command of a man that didn't know what it was to hang tough and hold a position. To hell with green captains and gourd-headed lieutenants!

Sergeant Wuestenhagen tried a number of times to surrender the company, but each time he climbed the hedgerow to wave the flag, he was invited to retreat in some haste, for the Krauts were not accepting a flag of truce and made their intentions quite clear by

Chapter 3. Fighting Two Wars

means of a machine gun that fired 1100 rounds per minute. When Captain O'Brien was thoroughly convinced that the Krauts were not in a mood to accept the company in a state of surrender, he gave the order to retreat further to the rear.

He called for volunteers to stay with the wounded, but I could not see any benefits to be gained by staying behind, only to be captured along with the wounded, so I told Dutch to stay with me and we would make it to the rear alone. I didn't like the orders Captain O'Brien was giving and took no chances in staying with the group of men that hung at his side. The sun went down, and darkness began to settle on the field where the wounded lay.

Dutch and I walked down the road that led to the rear. As I write this account, I cannot understand why the captain didn't take the wounded with him. There was no press in the attack and the Krauts didn't approach the field that he and his men had occupied while trying to surrender the company.

We met a contingent of the Tenth Armored Infantry Battalion that was coming to give us support but we didn't hesitate along the road to talk with them. We only asked if they had seen any of Company B as they hightailed it to the rear. They answered in the affirmative and we continued in the darkness until we reached our half-tracks, which had been left in a field a half mile to the rear of the front line.[4]

The next morning, when Company B was called together for a count, we discovered that at least half the company was either dead or taken captive. The men were very much shaken up over the previous day's action and most of them were grumbling among themselves that they were not going back on the line again, no matter what or who gave the order. I am prone to believe that it was shame that motivated the men to take this attitude, for I know that it was a shameful day's action on the part of the men of Company B. We had no leadership, and for this reason we were rebelling. It was a very sad and shameful day for the men of Company B.

As the day wore to evening, the men regained a little of their composure and began to move around a bit. I immediately set out, scouting by myself, in the hope I might get a shot at the prisoner the men said had escaped. Although I thought it to be only a rumor, I went about looking for him, very diligently. I was dressed in fatigues and a pair of black hobnailed boots that very definitely were not regulation. I could very easily have been mistaken for a Kraut, but at the time I was not aware of this fact.

I scouted around for thirty minutes or so and went back to the company. Someone had supposedly just seen the Kraut prisoner in the area from which I had just returned. Immediately, I knew it was I they had seen, and I dummied up, for I knew Captain O'Brien would surely be after my ass for the way I was dressed. I had picked up the black boots while in England and had worn them on pass because I had no dress shoes and didn't like the brogans the rest of the army was wearing. They looked too much like a bunch of farmers and I definitely did not like the idea of being one of them.

Lieutenant Duffy, the officer Doss had done in with four shots in the face, had repeatedly chewed my ass out for wearing the boots. The first day that we had spent in the apple orchard, where the Preacher got hit in the ass with a slug from Jim Cardone's rifle, Lieutenant Duffy called me to his half-track and gave me orders: get out of the boots. But now that Lieutenant Duffy was out of the picture, I slipped back into the boots and said, "To hell with all of them!"

I seemed to have been fighting two wars—one against the authority of a bunch of ring-tailed officers, who didn't know what they were doing, and another with the Krauts for whom I held no particular animosity. As a matter of fact, the only fear I felt was that of being taken prisoner. I had been thoroughly brainwashed from the very moment I entered the service. I had been taught to fear them rather than love them. I had been taught to send them to hell, with all dispatch.[5]

After the rumor of the escaped prisoner had died down, I hung my musette bag on the rail at the side of my half-track. I took my barracks bag and emptied it of all clean socks and underwear. I placed these articles in the musette bag and threw the barracks bag over the side of the track. All the unnecessary baggage went over the side. Too much bullshit, just like the man in the 4th Infantry Division told us. Too much bullshit and I was the first to take the hint. I

Chapter 3. Fighting Two Wars

A rear view of the M3A1 half-track (photograph by Don M. Fox).

was convinced that there would be some serious fighting going on and wanted to rig down for fast, mobile action. We rested for the remainder of that day and night. The next morning, we mounted our half-tracks and moved to a reserve position, waiting to be called back to the front to redeem whatever honor we may have had remaining.

The Krauts made a hard drive against a nearby infantry battalion, and we dismounted, moving into cover of darkness, to a position immediately to the rear of a company of this battalion.[6] It had been raining and the road was muddy as hell, like a hog pen. When we were a short distance behind the position under attack, we were ordered to dig in on the side of the muddy road. The next morning orders came down that the infantry battalion had successfully repelled the attack, and we were moved back to our former positions in reserve, where we waited.

On the morning of July 25 approximately three thousand bombers from the 8th Air Force gathered in the skies over Normandy. When the lead B-17 reached the target area near St. Lo, it dropped a smoke bomb, which left a trail in the skies like a finger, pointing down to the doomed landscape. As the bombs began to find their way, a continuous rumble of their explosions came to our attention, some five miles from where they struck. The earth began to tremble and the very grass around us shook as though some unseen force was approaching, causing each blade to tremble in fear. The Kraut anti-aircraft guns began to speak with some authority, and when their reports started homing in on the aircraft above us, the B-17s started dropping aluminum foil to befuddle the radar-directed cannon.[7]

Douglas A–20 bombers in action over France (U.S. Army photograph).

One of the craft dropped very slowly from the formation and went into a steep dive, trailing smoke. It fell for some distance, and then a giant puff of black smoke mixed with orange flame declared the death of all aboard. Still, the aircraft kept coming on. When the last bomb had fallen, the fighter planes came down at tree level over our position, strafing and bombing the enemy to our immediate front.

The order came to us for Company B to mount up and move out. Now we knew why they had held us in reserve. We had been waiting for the strategists to gather their forces for a final and conclusive assault against the enemy, who had held the Normandy coast far too long.[8]

Chapter 4

Leaving the Hedgerows Behind

As we moved out of the hedgerows onto the main road that led to Coutances, we passed through a village which had been bombed and pounded by our artillery until there was not a single building left standing. Destruction was on all sides and the enemy had ceased to exist as a combined force. They were completely disorganized by the devastating hail of death that rained down upon them from above. The 8th Air Force had broken the back of Hitler's resistance in Normandy. Now it was time for the steel tine of armor to be rammed through the heart of what remained of his fleeing forces.

The 4th Armored Division of which I was part rolled out on the road like a giant anaconda and lay there for the space of half an hour, waiting for all the machines of war to gather behind the head. When they were all in position, we were ordered to move in a frontal assault on the Brest Peninsula. The town of Coutances was the first city to be delivered into the hands of our division. However, before we came to this city, we met straggling forces of the German 7th Army, making haste to depart the fields of Normandy and leaving in much disorder that could be called a rout.[1]

We had been on the road a very short time when the column stopped to clear it of mines and a vehicle that had been knocked out of action. I looked across a field and saw a group of German soldiers, running down a road about two or three hundred yards away. I very quickly jumped from the half-track and raced straight across the field in the direction of the fleeing soldiers. I came to the road, where they had been running, but I could see no enemy. I returned to the

The city of Saint-Lô was pulverized during the battle for Normandy. Air bombardments caused much of the destruction (U.S. Army photograph).

A column of the Fourth Armored Division advances through Coutances. In the foreground is a M7 self-propelled howitzer of the 66th Armored Field Artillery Battalion. At the left rear, a M5 light tank from the Fourth Armored was disabled by an enemy mine (U.S. Army photograph).

Chapter 4. Leaving the Hedgerows Behind

half-track, and in short order the column started moving in the direction of Coutances and the Brest Peninsula.[2]

That night we moved off the road into a field, and as we passed through a gap in the fence, General Wood, the division commander, was standing at the gap, directing traffic.[3] He was waving his hand back and forth in a frenzied motion, making us realize that he wanted all the tracks off the road in a hell of a hurry. Moving into the field, someone shouted in a very loud voice, "There he is! Over there in that tree!" Somebody in a track behind us turned a machine gun around to the direction of

Major General John S. Wood, the commanding general of the Fourth Armored Division (U.S. Army photograph).

the tree and let loose with a burst of fire. A sniper, who had fired several shots into the column, fell from a limb in the tree and plummeted to the ground like a flying squirrel. He was a dead man before he hit.

The next morning, we moved on to the town of Coutances and found that we had flanked the enemy, for there was no resistance as we moved through the city. Its citizenry lined both sides of the main street, all hailing us as we passed, "Vive le American! Vive le American!"[4]

While they continued to shout their gratitude, several of us engaged in a poker game in the back of our half-track, building up

The seating inside the M3A1 half-track. There were seats for 10 infantrymen in the rear area. This restored M3A1 is part of the World War II Armor collection (photograph by Don M. Fox).

quite a large pot with the French money that had been issued to us before our arrival there. The betting continued until Dutch's bankroll was completely exhausted. Then came the moment of truth. Turning the cards up on a ration box we used for a table, Dutch realized I had beaten him fair and square, and shouting "bullshit" as loud as he could, he grabbed the money and threw it into the air.

The money fluttered down behind the half-track. When the Frenchmen became aware of what was happening, they rushed into the street behind our vehicle and began gathering the money. The column behind us was forced to slow down to prevent hitting the Frenchmen who were running in front of them, gathering the fallen currency. The local people didn't seem to notice the tracks coming on, and when we saw with what enthusiasm they gathered something upon which we placed little or no value, we all began throwing money into the air, shouting, "Viva le American! Viva le American!"

We took positions on a hill overlooking Coutances. We were scarcely settled when a group of thirty-odd fighter-bombers of the

Chapter 4. Leaving the Hedgerows Behind

Luftwaffe flew over our scattered division, dropping bombs and using rockets against our tanks that were covering the surrounding terrain. Every machine gun in the division opened on the group of aircraft, and in very short time, managed to knock about half of them from the sky.[5]

I remember very well one particular aircraft. Its pilot, deeming it wise to vacate that part of the country, made it to a spot just beyond the rim of the division. He must have realized that his craft wasn't going to carry him much farther before it blew up, for he dropped his remaining bombs, rolled the craft over, and bailed out. Spotting him floating toward the earth, his parachute supporting him on his way down, somebody with a .50 caliber machine gun opened up on him and dealt him much misery before he hit terra firma. I don't know whether or not they hit him, but before he struck ground, they made that noble gentleman know he had tangled with a cobra.

During all this action I was in a bomb crater, looking with much enthusiasm at the vast amount of lead that took to the air from the surrounding terrain, where the machines of war were mounted. There and then, I conceded that it took a brave enemy to tangle with that division of armor. Each vehicle mounted three to eight machine guns, and with the supporting anti-aircraft weapons, there was a veritable wall of fire being sent in the direction of the buzzing aircraft.

As I sat there on the rim of the bomb crater, gazing into the sky, one of the bombers flew over our position and sent a bomb hurtling toward the earth, end over end. Fifty feet from where I watched, it struck the ground with a resounding explosion of energy that blew me from the rim of the crater to its bottom, where I landed on my ass with a jar. I very quickly came to my feet, and, crawling out of the crater, hurried to the spot where the bomb had struck.

A piece of the bomb casing had landed a few feet away. I reached down and picked it up. I dropped it very quickly; it was exceedingly hot. There must have been one hell of a fire when that bomb exploded. After that, I touched no more bomb fragments.

The next morning, we mounted up again and proceeded in the direction of Avranches which is on the northern rim of the Brest Peninsula. Late that evening, we took positions along the

M5 light tanks from the Fourth Armored Division approach Avranches (U.S. Army photograph).

side of the road, well in concealment, for we were told that remnants of the German 7th Army would be moving down through us later.[6]

We didn't know how much later, but later, the next morning at daylight, a Blackfoot Indian in our company shot and killed the driver of a truck filled with German infantrymen. Being dead, the driver failed to answer the call of the bend in the road that led safely down the mountainside, and the truck plummeted earthward, German infantrymen flying in all directions. End over end, side over side, down the mountain, hands and feet, machine guns, loose equipment, rifles, and helmets, all flying in the breeze, as they came tumbling down the mountain.

We had been given specific orders not to fire, for our artillery had been in position since the evening before and zeroed in on the road that led down the mountainside. What the general had planned would have worked very well had it not been for the goddamn Indian's shooting of the driver of that truck. After that first shot broke

Chapter 4. Leaving the Hedgerows Behind

the stillness, all that could be heard was the rumbling of the truck as it crashed down the mountain.

A voice came out of the air and broke the stillness like the cry of a coyote on the desert floor. "Stop that goddamn truck!"

The voice broke off as suddenly as it had begun, and then, all hell broke loose. The German column stopped and dismounted right in the middle of town. There were only 80-odd men left to defend our positions in Company B, but defend it we did.

Ivy platoon, the third, was on one side of the road, and the second platoon was on the other side. The first platoon was in position a quarter of a mile to our rear, dug in as a reserve unit in a field. The company commander was with the first platoon.

As the German troops dismounted, all guns were fixed on them. During the following three or four hours, we didn't know whether we would live to tell the tale or go the way of the driver of the truck. I took up a position in the corner of a field that overlooked a sunken farm road, which was about 15 feet in width, with brush and saplings on either side. Within a few minutes after the first burst of fire, I looked across the road and spotted about ten German soldiers. They were coming across the field straight toward me. I raised my carbine and fired a clip into them. I dropped the weapon and started sailing hand grenades across the road into the spot they had hit ground, just behind the brush and only fifteen feet from where I lay, pulling the pins from the grenades, and getting rid of them as fast as I possibly could. I ran out of grenades and called for help.

Very soon, Kovacs the mortar man came running to my side with a bag full of grenades. We started tossing them over the road. When we stopped throwing the grenades, the Krauts across the road began firing small arms in our direction. I can still see the leaves from the overhanging trees, falling, as the bullets cut their way through the limbs.

Very soon, they slipped away from their position and went into a farmhouse about 150 feet away. I don't know how many of them did not make it to the farmhouse, for Kovacs and I had spilled some 25 grenades across the road before they left.

Things were quiet in my corner now, as I looked around to see how the other men were doing. Behind me were two men who had dug themselves in a trench when the action started. They had frozen up in the hole and were unable to protect themselves. Fear kept them frozen as I witnessed a German soldier appear on the hedgerow, looking down into their hole. After standing there for a fraction of time, he pulled the pin on a concussion grenade and dropped it into their hole. After the explosion of the grenade, I saw the two men come rolling out of the hole, holding their legs as they were screaming and moaning. They rolled over and over across the field, and I broke out into a laugh I could not control.

Sergeant Boeck, my squad leader, was in a position across the field when he saw what was going on. He snatched the machine gun he had been firing into a house and very quickly turned it around. Holding the barrel of the gun in one hand, he fired directly over the heads of the two men, who had vacated the hole, and the Kraut tumbled down into the same hole he had just tossed the grenade in. Little did those two boys realize they had been digging a grave the night before. Now a Kraut lay very still in a hole in the ground of a small town called Avranches, where a Blackfoot Indian fired the first shot at a German truck driver and cost us another 25 or 30 men from Company B.

When the fighting was over, Dutch and I unhitched a team of horses from a buggy that a Kraut had been making it south in and the two of us rode down a road in the direction of the command post. About two hundred yards to the rear of the position we fought so hard to protect, we came across 15 Russian soldiers who were dressed in German uniforms.

We didn't realize they were Russian at first. But when we dismounted and engaged them in conversation, one of them, speaking in French, told us that they were glad we came along, for they had been forced to join the German campaign. He explained further that all the men of his company were Russian, save the non-coms and the officers. He was so happy to see us that he cried as he related his story.[7]

As I look back on that particular day, I recall many events that stand out in my mind so vividly that it would be very difficult to

Chapter 4. Leaving the Hedgerows Behind

The Fourth Armored Division fought against non–Germanic units on more than one occasion. The soldiers were typically captives from the Eastern Front pressed into service by the *Wehrmacht* (U.S. Army photograph).

erase them, even if it served a worthwhile purpose to do so. I specifically recall a little feller by the name of Capo, one of my machine gun squad members, standing against a hedgerow, looking across the field beyond the road, where the German soldiers approached my concealed position when the fighting started. Apparently, we had wounded a German with the grenades we tossed, and now he lay in the field, some fifty yards from where Capo stood. He must have been wounded very badly, for he was unable to reach a farmhouse just a short distance from where he lay. A German medic would run from the house to the man in the field, as Capo observed with mischief in his heart. The medic would stoop down and engage his services for a while, and then run, hell bent for election, to the house, where there were fifteen or twenty of his comrades. Capo watched him for some time and became weary of the medic's action. He laid his rifle, which was as tall as he, over the hedgerow before him. Looking quietly down the barrel for a second, he pulled the trigger. The rifle barked and Capo jerked as though he had been kicked by a mule. The bullet struck the medic, sending him to kingdom come before he knew what hit him. Capo drew the rifle down off the hedgerow and set the stock at his feet. He drew his thumb across the end of his tongue and kicked the memory of that dead man off the front sight of his rifle forever. He looked around to see if anyone had noticed his accomplishment, and he saw me watching. He smiled and went about the business of guarding his position.[8]

There was another young feller of our platoon killed in that day's action, but I cannot recall his name for the life of me. He was a tall boy, very slim and easy-going. Wore glasses, to the best of my memory. Came from the state of Missouri and never had too much of importance to say. But on this day, he acquitted himself proudly and his memory will not escape me.

My squad leader, Sergeant Boeck, was in the immediate vicinity of the position held by this boy during the fighting. And when the fighting was over, it was told that the boy pulled the pin on a pineapple grenade and raised his arm to throw it when he was hit by a bullet focused on him from the house to which the medic would run. He was killed instantly and fell to the ground, grenade still in hand. But the release handle had not been freed.

Now after the fighting had stopped, Sergeant Boeck came upon the young feller, and without stopping to think, he stooped over him and took the grenade from his hand. He then slipped it into his own right rear pocket, which action freed the release handle. When the fuse capped and began to spew, Sergeant Boeck realized what he had done and immediately reached into the nest of his rear pocket to remove the deadly egg. The handle of the grenade had sprung to an open position and caught on the lip of his pocket, refusing to be freed.

He wrestled with the grenade frenziedly, with the thought of death racing through his mind, and fear clenched in his teeth. The grenade went off, blowing Sergeant Boeck's hand from its task, scattering most of it to the four winds, and gouging a chunk of flesh out of his right buttock, the size of a helmet liner. When he reached the states, he wrote me a letter, saying he was all right. I am confident that if Sergeant Boeck is alive today, he would laugh at Hollywood when they blow up bridges and tanks, and houses, and their minds with World War II grenades.

Joe Kiernan was a tall, thin, intellectual comic who was at the

Chapter 4. Leaving the Hedgerows Behind

same time a good cartoon artist. He had a good sense of humor and livened the day when he felt up to it. On this same day he was goosed in the ribs with a rifle held by the hands of a very determined soldier from the Wehrmacht, who surprised Kiernan and caught him red handed. The German soldier was marching the boy down the street, with his hands over his head in a position of give-up, when the two of them came to a field, just at the edge of town, where the second platoon of our company held some 650 surrendered German prisoners. Kiernan immediately dropped his hands and turned on his captor, who readily appreciated his position, and Joe accepted the rifle with which he had been captured. The Kraut cooperated to the fullest extent. The two of them walked into the field. The German disappeared among his comrades and Kiernan went about the business of rejoining his squad to continue for another day.[9]

Two days later, my company pulled off the road some distance

German prisoners under guard by members of the 25th Armored Cavalry Reconnaissance Squadron, Fourth Armored Division (U.S. Army photograph).

A M4 Sherman tank moves through the city of Avranches (U.S. Army photograph).

south of Avranches and bivouacked in an orchard. Late in the evening, I took three men from my squad, and we walked some 300 yards to a farmhouse. We walked into the front yard, and I knocked on the door. I was hoping to make a deal for some butter and eggs, or anything else that might be available. I glanced to my left and saw a German helmet with a very live German head inside, peering over a wagon bed some distance from the house. I turned very casually to the men and knocked on the door again, speaking in a very low tone, "Turn around and walk toward the road and don't ask any questions. There's a German soldier over behind that wagon. Don't act like you see anything and don't look in his direction. Just get the hell out of here."

We all turned at the same time and strolled very casually in the direction of "away," never once looking back. Nothing was said of the incident when we returned to the platoon. None of us knew how many of them may have been in the bushed area behind the wagon, and we didn't want any ninety-day wonder trying to make a name for himself at our expense.

We said nothing. We avoided a fight. We lived in peace for another day. The Kraut went his way, and I went mine. I'll never know whether or not he was aware that I was aware of his presence.

Chapter 5

Don't Mess with a Dragon

The next day we approached the city of Rennes, which is on the Brest Peninsula, a hundred miles south of the town of Avranches.[1]

The division pulled up before the city and halted while the commander of the task force made up his mind what strategy he would use to capture same. It was decided that he would deploy the armor around the city to guard the roads leading out and use a contingent of the 8th Infantry Division for a frontal assault in an attempt to push the Krauts out of the city.[2]

The third platoon, with five half-tracks and a tank from the 8th Tank Battalion, were sent around the city to guard one of the blacktop road exits against any efforts of escape by the entrapped soldiers of the German Army that was encamped within the city.

We took up a position outside the city, where the blacktop road was crossed by a dirt road, five miles behind their line. Here, from atop a long grade that sloped into the city, we commanded a view of the blacktop road. The tank held the middle of the road just over the military slope of the hill, capable of assuming a firing position to bring hellfire down on any encroaching enemy.[3] We set a bazooka team at the crossroad and patiently waited for the 8th Infantry Division to make their push against the entrapped enemy.

Late in the evening, the 8th I.D. made a drive and the Krauts came spilling out of the city in all directions. Evidently, they had been trying to recuperate from the battle fought in Avranches and were running out of ammunition, for their column approaching the road guarded by my platoon had no artillery or anti-tank weapons at their disposal.

You're a Good Man, Sergeant

A half-track from the 53rd Armored Infantry Battalion advances south from Normandy. The M3A1 half-track was an integral part of the battalion, with each "track" carrying a squad of infantrymen. It was also common for the infantry to ride atop the division's tanks (U.S. Army photograph).

At approximately 10:00 o'clock in the evening a convoy approached the crossroads, where we waited, and came to a stop about fifty yards before reaching our position. He waited quietly. A soldier with hobnailed boots jumped out of his vehicle and engaged another in conversation for the space of a minute. He returned to his vehicle, and, having left the motor running, he released the brake and stepped on the accelerator. This proved to be the last thing that this gentleman did while he was still in possession of his faculties, for Simonazzi, one of the bazooka team, cut down on that lead vehicle, a gasoline truck, and sent a missile through the cab into the tank which immediately burst into flame. It literally exploded, lighting the countryside with a brightness that could be seen for miles. The tank moved into position and began to fire directly into the column from point-blank range.[4]

The five half-tracks of the third platoon, complete with the machine gun squad, were lined up at the crossroads. When Simonazzi hit the lead vehicle with the bazooka missile, all five

Chapter 5. Don't Mess with a Dragon

The M3A1 half-track. This excellent example of the workhorse of the armored division resides in the collection of the organization World War II Armor. The ring-mounted .50 caliber M2 machine gun was a potent weapon. Variants of the machine gun are still in use today (photograph by Don M. Fox).

.50 caliber machine guns opened with such a stream of fire that the entire sky was lit up from the tracers.

There were about 26 of us left after the battle at Avranches, and every man concentrated unceasing fire in the direction of the column for no less than fifteen minutes, and then sporadically for another thirty-odd minutes. Then, all was very still. The exploding truck had sent its fragments in all directions, scattering flame into the surrounding area, which kept burning until well past midnight.

In the early morning hours, a twin-engine bomber we'd given the name "Bed Check Charlie" circled the area for a while and left. By dawn I was exhausted and dozed off into a deep slumber in a ditch. When I awoke and looked down the ditch, I saw a German soldier, lying flat on his stomach with a concussion grenade in his hand. We just looked at each other for a moment or two. He rose up out of the ditch, dropped the grenade, and raised his hands over his head in a state of surrender. He was a young feller and offered no resistance at all when I ran my hands over him, shaking him down for concealed weapons.

He spoke perfect English. He told me that he had a comrade in a field just a short distance away. He further explained that his comrade wanted to surrender but would not for fear of getting shot. He asked me to go with him to get his comrade. We walked down the blacktop road about 75 yards, where he stepped up on an embankment and called out to his fellow soldier. He assured him that we were all right and there was nothing to fear. The hidden German raised up out of the tall grass of the field and walked toward us, saying nothing but looking very much concerned.

The three of us went back to my half-track and the young feller explained to me that there were many more of his comrades down the road about a quarter of a mile from our position who wanted to surrender if they could get someone to go with him to accept their surrender. I asked Simonazzi, the bazooka man, to accompany me, and the three of us walked down the blacktop road in the direction of the city of Rennes.

When we were within a hundred yards of the men who wanted to surrender, Simonazzi and I walked down into the ditches on either side of the road and instructed the young German soldier to tell his comrades we would await their decision.

He walked down the road to where a group of his men were standing and spoke with them for some time. He stepped away from them and shouted for us to approach. Simonazzi and I climbed out of our ditches and walked down the middle of the road, where we could see that a number of the local people had gathered with the German soldiers and were talking to them. He spoke with the young German soldier for a short time. He told us they all wanted to surrender. I crawled behind the wheel of a Mercedes-Benz one of them had been driving, and Simonazzi sat on the top resting his feet on the cowling. He instructed two of the prisoners to sit on the front fenders and the balance of them to march before the car up the hill. He gave them into the hands of our fellow soldiers and went back down the hill, where the French people still gathered on the road.

I took a small automobile that had been abandoned by the

Chapter 5. Don't Mess with a Dragon

German troops and drove it to the top of the hill, where I presented it to a French captain, who had relieved himself of the responsibility of fighting the war with the men of the French 7th Army. He was so proud of that gesture and so grateful for the gift that he caught me full on both cheeks with the customary French kiss of brotherly love and recognition. The French people gathered around our positions and brought us bread, butter, and eggs. They stood around us for some time, just looking at us, for we were the first Americans they had seen.

There was a house at the corner of the crossroads, with an open well in the front yard. The commander of the tanks took a jerry-can and walked down to the well for a supply of fresh water. The well was rigged with a windlass type device and the rope was already let out to the bottom of the well. The lieutenant took hold of the windlass handle and proceeded to crank the bucket to the top. He told us later that he thought the bucket to be awfully heavy but didn't know why until the bucket had reached the top of the well. As the rope wound around the spool and drew the bucket to the top, the lieutenant asked why the bucket had been so heavy.

Hanging on to the bucket, before the lieutenant's startled eyes was a young German soldier who had slid down the rope the night before, when all the fireworks had started. The man had spent the entire night hanging on to the well rope, and had the commander of the tank not thought of replenishing his water supply, the young feller could very easily have died, hanging at the end of the same rope that had saved his life.

We left our positions and two days later set up an outpost at another crossroad, some 75 miles outside a town where submarines were based.[5] Our position was at the end of a dirt road that was perpendicular to another, forming a "T." We were not too near any town or village. We sat at the dead end for a day or two, with a machine gun aimed straight down the center of the road we were guarding.

As I sat behind the machine gun, I noticed a small black automobile with a steam tank atop, trailed by a rising cloud of dust. It was coming at a very fast clip toward the position I held. At first, I thought to open up on it, but something inside me told me to hold my fire. As the vehicle approached, I stepped in front of the machine gun and halted it. The three men that crawled out of the car were from the Free French of the Interior. They had commandeered the automobile and were on their way to get two French girls who had been fraternizing with the German staff officers occupying their area.

The three men were awfully excited and seemed in a hell of a hurry to get the two girls, but I held them at the crossroads long enough to make a swap with one of them. I noticed they were wearing American sidearms at their belts. One of them carried a Smith and Wesson .44 caliber pistol and another had a Colt .45 Shooting Master strapped around his waist. I wanted those pistols in the worst way, and had it not been for one of my squad mates, I'd have made the trade for both. They were carrying weapons which had been dropped to them by the English and were running short of ammunition, so it was not too difficult to make the trade. I wound up with the Colt .45 Shooting Master, and Blackie, my second gunner, made the swap for the .44.

The Frenchmen disappeared down the road. We waited for their return. Approximately half an hour later, the little black car came hurtling back to our position and stopped. The three of them got out of the car, dragging two very young girls behind them. They couldn't have been more than fifteen or sixteen years old. Both had been cropped to the skull. I should imagine sheep shears were used for the task, for their hair was very gapped and crudely cut, allowing sections of their heads to reveal scalp. The Frenchmen offered the girls to us so that we might make sport of them, but we declined. We were not given to taking girls against their own wishes, or when we held them prisoner. Even though they had been shacked up with the Kraut officers, it didn't seem right to dishonor them any further.

We told the Frenchmen we would pass. They pulled the girls back in the car, lit the furnace attached to the bumper, and struck down the road in the direction from which they had come. God only knows what punishment befell the young girls, but I suppose they took them to a village, where they stripped them of their clothes and paraded them through the streets to shame them, for this was their custom.

Chapter 5. Don't Mess with a Dragon

Other than that one incident, nothing very much transpired while we held that position. But before we left, I discovered why we had been guarding that crossroad. We hadn't been informed when we were outposted there, but upon taking a walk it became clear to me. As I walked down the dusty road, a German Shepherd, looking as big as a polo pony, ran up on an embankment on the left side of the road and opened his mouth in much protest at my presence. I turned in his direction, looked at him momentarily, and without taking the .45 out of its holster, I raised the muzzle and pulled the trigger. The bullet struck him in the right shoulder, and he let out a yell.

Tucking his tail between his legs, he ran off through the woods, holding his right leg up. The slug from the .45 knocked all the mean out of him, and he came to recognize the authority that stood before him. That was one soldier that didn't get the Purple Heart for his action that day. He had been guarding an ammunition dump, and his fellow soldiers had run out on him and left the dog alone.

We left that position and for three days traveled across France, running into spotted resistance in three small towns. When we did run into resistance the tanks would fire several rounds into the town and we, the armored infantry, would dismount and proceed into the town, which was usually empty when we got there. There wasn't too much willingness on the part of the enemy to resist the armor that lay stretched out before him like a giant snake.

The division had been split into three combat commands, and each of the commands splintered into task forces, which moved against the villages or small cities in the wine country.[6] Company B was riding the point, with a tank from the 8th Tank Battalion leading the way.[7] The column of armor stretched out on the blacktop road like an armored Chinese dragon, and as the lead tank crawled around a curve in the road, a Kraut snapped the lanyard on an "88" and the round drilled a one-inch hole squarely between the dragon's eyes. The driver of the tank was killed instantly, and his assistant was badly wounded. The commander of the tank leaped to the assistant driver's hatch, and, reaching down and taking hold of the wounded man, he drew his bleeding frame through the hole and dropped him into the arms of the gunner and his assistant. The three of them carried the wounded tanker back around the curve and laid him on the medic's jeep, which disappeared down the road. That tanker done got himself a ticket to the United States.

The Krauts had an anti-aircraft gun mounted on four wheels sitting in the middle of the street. It had a barrel as long as a telephone pole and the artillery piece had been pointed on the curve of the road before we arrived on the scene. When the dragon stuck his head around the curve, the Kraut gunner blew a hole in his head.

Within a few short minutes the dragon grew, boasting three heads to replace the one that had been killed. The commander of the force barked out a quick set of orders, and the third platoon took off through a grape vineyard to the right of the column, while the second platoon loped off the road to the left. The village at the bottom of the hill was about to be hit by three heads of the Chinese dragon.

I ran through the grape vineyard with the tripod of a .30 caliber machine gun on my hump. I came out of the vineyard into an open field that was scattered with manure heaps. I ran hard, as a Kraut counterpart played "Turkey in the Straw" on an angry machine gun in the valley below. By the time I reached the middle of the field, I had the tripod opened and slammed it down on top of one of the dung heaps. Blackie, my second gunner, dropped the gun on the tripod and I saddled 'er up, jerked the bolt back and slammed a round home.

The machine was riding free in the cradle and the tracers led the nose, which was poking right into the middle of a bunch of Krauts who were running from a house, trying to board a bus that was supposed to carry them to the land of milk and honey. The tracers leaped out of the nose of the machine gun, playing around the house and yard where the Krauts were running to the bus. The entire area was filled with a "nest of hornets on the prod." The Kraut was boiling over the pot, running in all directions, while the dragon's head spewed smoke and fire from his nose—and pure death from his roaring, angry mouth.

"Porter, you son-of-a-bitch! Hold your fire! Hold your fire! Hold your fire," the voice of Lieutenant Green, who was behind a tree twenty yards in the back of me, spilled into the ears of a deaf dragon.

Chapter 5. Don't Mess with a Dragon

Erik Albertson of the organization World War II Armor demonstrates the operation of a .30 caliber Browning M1919A4 light machine gun, the weapon used by Porter's light machine gun squad (photograph by Don M. Fox).

And the fiddle just kept playing. "Porter!!! goddamn you! Hold your fire!"[8]

I grabbed another box of ammunition and jerking the bolt cover open and laying a fresh belt into the breech, I slammed the cover and jerked the bolt back to slide one rounder into the hornets' nest. The gun was smoking hot, and the dance had just begun to warm up.

"Porter!!! Hold your fire! That's the second platoon! Hold your goddamn fire!"

I paid no attention and went about my business, blasting away at what Lieutenant Green said was the second platoon.

"Porter, goddamn you! That's the second platoon! Hold that goddamn fire!"

The dragon was still deaf.

Lieutenant Green raised his rifle to his shoulder and laid 'er down, with the muzzle pointing at me. Dutch, my Polish sidekick, saw what Lieutenant Green was about to do and slapped the rifle out of his hand. "What's the matter with you, Green?" he barked, as the lieutenant looked around. "Goddamit, them's Krauts out there!"

Green had yelled his damn fool head off, trying to tell me that the men I had been firing on were the men of the second platoon. But I knew he was full of bullshit, just like most of them were, when a good hot dance, to the tune of Sally Goodin, got started.[9] The second platoon hadn't even had time to get into the village and I knew it. The second platoon wouldn't be trying to board a bus and I knew it. The second platoon didn't wear gray uniforms and bobbed-off helmets. I knew this, also. The second platoon wouldn't have fired at me as I ran across the open field to the dung heap. I knew this, too. Lieutenant Green was a former sergeant in Lieutenant Luxbacher's antitank platoon and used to hobnob with Luxbacher, who was also full of shit, and this I knew.

We finally picked up our gear and walked down the hill toward the village, passing a wounded Kraut at the side of the trail we followed. He had been one of the fellers that failed to make it to the bus and had tried to crawl away from the village, bleeding from the gut.

A wounded German soldier receives aid from American troops (U.S. Army photograph).

Chapter 5. Don't Mess with a Dragon

As we passed him, he asked for a drink of water. One of the less charitable of our gang spit at him. I can't recall who it was, but whoever it was, he was a dumb bastard. When we reached the center of the village, it became quite obvious that we, the third platoon, were the first to occupy it. The second platoon came into the town more than fifteen minutes later. Thanks, Green, you big asshole.

The bus was still sitting in the backyard, riddled with holes, and a few of its would-be passengers stayed in town—quite a few of them in fact—to watch the dragon snake its way through the main street. Some of them were never to rise again. They were dead men, who would try to catch the devil's herd, riding through the sky.

Chapter 6

Wine, Women and Troyes

Once again, the third platoon was dispatched for outpost duty. We traveled for three hours before coming to a halt at a crossroad outside the city of Blois which is on the river Loire. It must have been 11:00 p.m. before we had staked out this intersection, then we all went to sleep, posting a guard throughout the night. The next morning at daybreak, we discovered we had parked well within the limits of a city the size of Albuquerque, and a crowd of the local citizenry had gathered around our half-tracks, eager to take a look at their American liberators.[1]

After some chitchat with the people, I singled out one of them who patronized one of the busier bistros, and rounded up the squad, leaving John Rice, a well-intentioned man from Baltimore, on the half-track while ten of us cut out to make our presence known at the house of red lights.[2]

As we walked through the front door, the girls did drop the Free French of the Interior men, who had been sporting with them from an early morning hour, and with one accord began to shout, "Vive l'American, Vive l'American!" The Frenchmen disappeared and we took the house into our possession. I picked out a blonde I thought was capable of taking away the cares of the war and took her to a room upstairs, but I didn't keep her too long. I went back downstairs and selected a good-looking brunette, who looked as though she might have a little more spirit than the blonde and climbed back upstairs. I don't like to talk about ladies, but that particular lady sure knew her trade, and before the day was out, she had me in a position where I didn't care whether there was war or peace outside. I just didn't care.

Chapter 6. Wine, Women and Troyes

Blackie ran out of money and began stealing wine and cognac, hiding the bottles in my raincoat which I had left hanging in the parlor on the door. It was an officer's dress coat with a zip-out lining. I told the girls goodbye, and when I left, lifting the coat off the door, it almost hit the floor. Blackie hadn't told me what he had done, and the weight of the coat caused my arm to sag. When I realized what had happened, I refrained from putting on the coat, for I knew the bottles would make a hell of a tinkling noise. So, I just held it in my hand until we were on the sidewalk in front of the house where we had made sport all day.

It had been a good day. Both of us were about half loaded. As we walked back to the half-track, we began to sing, "Roll Me Over in the Clover." We stopped at a wine shop for a last go at it before we hit the straw. We had only a few drinks, then left. We went to the half-track, where we slept soundly for the first time in many a day.

The next morning, we went to the winery that we'd been in the previous night, only to find that a German tank across the river had laid an "88" right through the front door and literally gutted the place. Blackie was still with me when I found my way to a chateau located on a very high cliff that commanded a very good view of both sides of the river which ran through the city. The Free French of the Interior had been firing across the river, where we later learned there were some 30,000 German troops who had blown up the bridge behind them as a defensive maneuver.

The French troops had only a couple of Sten guns and a few side arms that weren't too effective at such long range. We gave them a machine gun from the half-track and took the light guns away from the wall from which they had been firing. An "88" across the river had drilled a hole about three feet in diameter in that wall, and they had been firing the Sten gun through the opening. We instructed them to fire a few bursts from the machine gun and then move their position, for if they did not, the Krauts would spot them firing through the hole and send them another message via the "88." I tried the Sten gun but didn't like the blowback action of the bolt, and very quickly went back to the carbine I'd lifted from Lieutenant Duffy back in the hedgerows of Normandy.

We played around with the French troops for the better part of the day, firing at the Germans across the river but soon grew tired of that action, and began directing our fire at some flowerpots in a lady's window about fifty yards below the wall. The two of us had shot all the flowerpots out of the window before she showed up in the opening, trying to see what was going on. We changed the direction of our fire and concentrated it on a bunch of gargoyles on the front of a church building about 75 yards from the chateau. We soon grew tired of this, also, and went back to the half-track.

Later in the evening, we loaded up our gear and took out of Blois to rejoin the combat command which had been posted along the river, covering a distance of 50 to 75 miles.[3] At midnight, we came into a fairly large town that had been evacuated by the Germans, and a group of our men went into a rather nice hotel to discover that there had been a banquet there that night. Evidently, the German officers had been having themselves a ball, but when they found out we were entering the city, they cut out in a hurry, leaving half-filled bottles of wine along with the remains of their evening meal. The spread filled a room 60 feet long and 30 feet wide. We camped out in the street that night. The next morning, we mounted up and struck across country for the city of Strasbourg on the River Rhine.[4]

Some days later, we came into the German-occupied city of Troyes, and our lead vehicles engaged the enemy for about an hour outside the town before moving into the city. The defensive troops were crumbling and offered little resistance. When the lead vehicles engaged the Germans, our tracks had been further back in the column, just waiting, although we knew not for what.[5]

Finally, an order came down to us that we were to dismount and go to the lead vehicle. When we got there, there seemed to be a great deal of confusion going on between our company commander and a lieutenant he was trying to get to go to the library to secure some maps of the city. The lieutenant was reluctant to attempt the task and asked the company commander where the library was located. The commander, chewing the lieutenant's ass out, reported "Hellfire man! I don't know where the goddamn library is! Go find it!" The

Chapter 6. Wine, Women and Troyes

lieutenant lit out in his jeep, and to this day I do not know whether he found the library or not.[6]

Capo, the little Cuban from New York City, and I dispatched ourselves on a little scouting spree and began looking at the immediate part of the city. Capo, the man who had shot the medic at Avranches, and I crawled to the top of a three-story building and proceeded to scan the area. The most important target we could see was the company commander, standing on the street a block away. I didn't like that company commander worth a damn, and as we lay there on the roof, we discussed the possibility of doing him in. I drew down on his lower half and weighed the thought of pulling the trigger. I decided I could get myself in a hell of a lot of trouble by shooting our good captain. Then we thought we might just shoot him in the knee, but decided against that, too, and crawled back to the ground.

We went into another building, looking for anything of value, for we were prone to looting more than anything else. Finding nothing, we began looking into windows for German troops that might be in the area.

A block away, we found another good-sized building, with a board fence around it. I hoisted Capo to the top of the six-foot fence so that he might observe what was behind it. He informed me that on the other side there was a booby trap wire running along the fence about a foot off the ground. He went across the street, where we took a lady's wire clothesline. It was made of very heavy wire. We crooked one end of the line and walked back to the board fence. Capo had the crooked end of the line in his hand, as I lifted him to the top. He laid the crooked end over the booby trap wire and I let him down to the street. The two of us walked across the street, and just as I was about to jerk the line, a Frenchman came strolling down the street. I called to him, "Allez vous. Allez vous."

He kept walking, not paying any attention to the warning. I waited until he was directly in front of the fence and gave a hell of a jerk on the clothesline. The explosion from the attached mine behind the fence threw up a hell of a ball of smoke and dust into the air, rocking the fence forward and hurling it to the ground. The Frenchman took off down the street in such a hurry that his feet got to outracing his body, making one hell of a picture to be remembered. It appeared that the feet of this Frenchman were a good two feet out in front of the rest of his body. He was flat getting out of that territory.

Capo and I went through the opening in the fence and looked around the building for German troops. Finding none, we returned to the street, where the company commander was still in a state of confusion. We mounted up again and drove to a position in front of an eight-foot wall that held behind it a supply depot. The enemy was encamped inside.

The supply buildings covered an entire square block, and we were to learn later that the entire square was tunneled. At first my half-track and the anti-tank half-track took up positions directly in front of the supply depot. As a matter of fact, we were just across the street from the main gate of the depot. The anti-tank squad had their 57-millimeter cannon directed across the street and started to fire from less than 75 yards into the front of the supply depot buildings. The armor-piercing projectiles went through the brick walls, leaving holes some three feet in diameter, but there was no return fire. It grew dark and we spent the night sleepless,

A towed 57mm anti-tank gun being deployed in Aachen, Germany. This weapon was standard issue for the armored infantry battalions but proved of limited value due to its relatively weak firepower against heavier German armor (U.S. Army photograph).

Chapter 6. Wine, Women and Troyes

in front of the depot, waiting. We did not know what was going to happen.

The next morning, we moved our half-tracks around the corner and a block away to a position in the middle of the street. We also commanded the two side streets along the eight-foot wall that surrounded the supply depot. We mounted two of the machine guns on a tripod to cover the two side streets. Capo sat on the .50 caliber machine gun on the track and we waited to see what would happen.

The people living nearby began to stir around, making conversation with the American soldiers who had come to liberate their town. One of them sported long blonde hair and walked with a mince in her step. Her hair hung loose and made quite a picture to be beheld by a group of men who had been busy trying to stay alive and without much time for the fairer sex.

As she passed our position, I engaged her in conversation and made a date with her for later in the afternoon. She left and I waited patiently for her return. Later in the afternoon, a group of Frenchmen came down the street, with a woman running before them, and from all indications, they were very angry people. They jeered at her. As they approached my position, I recognized her to be the woman with whom I had made the date.

They had sheared her hair, leaving rough gaps all the way to the scalp. They had stripped her of her clothing, too. She was running naked through the streets of the city, being jeered at by a bunch of damn fools as she ran past them.

I said to myself, there goes my date. As I looked at that happening, I felt that the damn fools should have been stripped of their clothing and thrown over the fence that guarded the Heiney soldiers from our view. Maybe the Krauts would have raped the whole shebang. This is what they needed if you look at the situation in the clearest light. Self-righteous dogs, treating one of their own in that manner, when, if the truth were known, there wasn't one of them who hadn't done worse, only in another way.

But of course, those who boasted the black arm band of the Free French of the Interior were given to brutalizing when they had the upper hand. As they say in their native tongue, "C'est la vie."

I went into a house which stood at the corner of the street we were guarding, and from the second floor, I could see over the eight-foot wall. The Germans were dug in. They had dug a trench along the inside of the wall, and I could see them preparing to make war against us. I ran down a hall that divided the upstairs bedrooms and went out onto a balcony. Holding on to the door jamb with one hand and swinging forward, I was allowed the full view of the trench across the fence. I pulled the pins on a couple of grenades, and tossing them into the trench, I ran down the hall to a bedroom, where I heard the grenades explode. I tossed another grenade through the bedroom window, and then went back to the balcony. I tossed more grenades from the balcony and ran back to the bedroom.

From the bedroom I tossed another grenade, which was aimed at the trench, or so I thought. The grenade hit a bar, which acted as a guard rail on the window, and bounced back into the room with me. I looked down on the bed where the grenade landed, and very quickly began my exit from the room.

The door was partially blocked by the bed, leaving only the narrowest of openings, and the .45 pistol on my hip caught on the door, holding me too near the spewing grenade. I made a hard lunge against the obstructing door and the holster of the .45 came free, sending me plunging out into the hallway. The grenade went off and the explosion gave away my position. Looking up from the floor, I saw a line of holes being punched in the wall, about a foot above my head.

The Krauts had spotted my position and had turned a machine gun in my direction. They were busily engaged in an attempt to eliminate the cause of their uneasiness. I crawled to a window on the opposite side of the house, lifted myself off the floor, and swung out the window, hanging on to the window stool.

I hung there for a one full minute, while the men on the ground called out, "Drop, Porter! Drop!"

But I was on the second floor and couldn't get ready for such a fall. As I hung there, the owner of the house looked out the window and gazed down at me, making me feel like a damn fool. He extended his hand, which I did not hesitate to accept, and he pulled me back through the window. I looked at him for a moment, then hit

Chapter 6. Wine, Women and Troyes

the staircase in a hell of a rush to get out of there. Evidently, he didn't know what I had been doing up there. I know he wasn't aware that I had blown one of his bedrooms to shambles with the misplaced grenade. I left him standing there and rejoined the squad on the street below. There would be no amour in the bed that night.

I took over the machine gun on the sidewalk and lay there for some time, looking at a group of men as they ran from the gate in the fence to across the street, and then back again. I soon became aware that they were German soldiers, coming out in civilian clothes and bringing civilian clothes back to their comrades. They thought they might make the short distance across the street before we realized what was happening. I called to a group of them, "Allez! Allez!" But they continued to run across the street, as if nothing was happening.

I unloosed the mechanism that held the gun in a fixed position and pulled back on the trigger, sending a hell of a hailstorm down the street in their midst. The gun sent hot steel in their direction, swinging freely back and forth, and then the confusion stopped. There was no one left in the street. It eliminated the confusion of having to look too closely at the garb that was the mode of the day.

When this incident died away, I turned the gun to face down the other street and waited. In a few minutes, I noticed the limbs of a tree, which stood about fifteen feet from the corner of the fence, begin to shake. The leaves rattled and I waited. Then a young German soldier swung out of the tree and dropped over the fence, just fifteen feet from 13 fully armed men who were spoiling for a chance to make war. He immediately threw his hands over and around his neck, fingers entwined, to show he would not contest the issue.

Moments later, a comrade of his dropped to the street and pressed the panic button. He turned and broke into a dead run down the street, never realizing what grief he had caused his partner, for the first bullet fired hit the young man in a state of surrender, square between the eyes and felled him like a tree. Then, every gun in the squad turned to direct their fire on the back of the fleeing soldier. The impact of the connecting bullets, as they struck him in the back, only served to speed him down the street.

He ran halfway down the block and turned into a garage, where

The .30 caliber Browning M1919A4 light machine gun (photograph by Don Fox).

he caught one of our platoons by surprise. Not realizing that the German soldier was bleeding from more than a dozen wounds, our man, caught with his gun away from him in a corner, threw up his hands and surrendered to the German, but the German fell to the man's feet. The American felt very foolish and the Kraut was kaput. C'est la guerre.

The mortar squad set up a tube about two blocks in front of the compound we had been guarding and began to bring them under fire. The 57-millimeter anti-tank gun, which had been firing into the front of the building, continued until there was nothing left of the front of the building which had once housed the wares that had been lifted from the French. In the early afternoon hours, the enemy decided the cause was lost and raised a white flag, sending out a man to inform us that they would surrender.

We sent the prisoners back to Division and occupied the compound, which proved to be very rich in food and clothing, most of which was civilian. Our only interest in the operation was clearing the streets of the enemy. After this was accomplished, I

Chapter 6. Wine, Women and Troyes

commandeered a motorcycle, and, removing the side car, rode through the streets, raising hell and showing my ass.

After some time, the company commander told me to get rid of the machine. I did. I went into a warehouse and took a case of cigarettes. I crawled atop the fence in front of the buildings and started throwing them to the French people below.

As the cigarettes hit the street, a crowd gathered, and like chickens, they began pecking for the weeds. I noticed two very good-looking girls standing back from the crowd, refusing to run after the cigarettes as the others did. When the cigarettes had all been thrown, I let myself down to the ground, walked over to the two girls, and engaged them in conversation. One of them allowed that I was a barbarian and told me so. She took no precaution to bite her tongue or mince her words. She evidently came from the higher echelon and didn't realize we were fighting a war—unless she was under the impression it was done with lace and fans rather than blood and guts. I laughed at them and went to the nearest barber shop.

After trading the French barber a pair of silk stockings I had taken from the warehouse for a haircut, I went in search of the sporting girls. To hell with the higher echelon!

Chapter 7

God Takes Care of Drunks and Fools

The next morning, we mounted up and rolled through the streets, which held groups of resistance spotted along the way. As we moved on, the entire column began firing across the canal. Somebody must have seen Germans on the other side. Seemed to be the thing to do, so I opened in the same direction with a .50 caliber I had mounted on the half-track; a gun I had retrieved from a shot down B-17 in a field outside the city of Troyes.

Now the barrel was bucking to the time of about 300 rounds per minute. We were moving about 40 miles per hour, as we were in much of a hurry to get past any resistance that offered fire power. We raced along the canal, with every gun in the convoy firing at the other side.

My eye caught a man running along the opposite bank, and before I realized who he was or what he was doing, I turned the gun in his direction and pulled back on the trigger. The gun started bucking and the man scrambled along the canal bank in a hell of a rush to get under something that would afford him relief from the deadly hail of fire biting at his tail. Within the space of five seconds, I had sent big lead, no less than fifteen pounds, on a mission of death that should never have begun, for something then snapped in my cranium, telling me I had been firing on an American soldier. Still can't figure out why he was there in the first place, but I guess he had business to attend to. Don't know whether I hit him or not.

One thing I do know, this gentleman was very uncomfortable for the space of five seconds. One of those unfortunate incidents of war

Chapter 7. God Takes Care of Drunks and Fools

that could not be avoided. Could have been that I was a little trigger happy.

We came to a halt, a mile or two west of the Moselle River, and waited for a contingent of the 80th Infantry Division to build a bridge.[1] After three or four days of just sitting there, I decided to go back to the hospital to be treated for a "running cold" I had contracted in a house of ill repute. I had been taking sulfa drugs to no avail and the red-headed major doctor had written out an order for me to be treated with penicillin at the field hospital.[2] The good doctor at the hospital gave me three shots in the keyster and told me I would have to stay another day for observation. I did not like the idea very much, so at four the next morning, when I heard a motor revving up outside the hospital tent, I slipped out of bed and approached an ambulance driver.

"What outfit you from, podner?"

"Fourth Armored," he replied.

I crawled in beside him and told him in no uncertain terms: "You've got a passenger, podner."

I got back to the company about an hour before an order came

Elements of the Fourth Armored Division fording the Moselle River (U.S. Army photograph). The jeep at the forefront carries the markings of the 22nd Armored Field Artillery Battalion.

down for us to cross the bridge that had been erected across the Moselle River.[3] The squad leaders had held a critique with the platoon lieutenants and were told that as soon as we passed through the small village just beyond the river, we were to place the tracks in a wedge formation behind a platoon of tank destroyers and attack an enemy-held position, a mile beyond the village.

The tank destroyers moved out onto the road in front of us and the column started moving in the direction of the bridge. As we approached the pontoon structure that our engineers had thrown across the river, General Wood, our division commander, stood beside the road, waving his arms at the drivers as they approached him, shouting, "Move it! Move it!"[4]

We crossed the bridge and moved about 200 yards toward the village. Then the column stopped.

I looked down from the half-track and saw an American soldier lying in a ditch, with his throat slit from ear to ear. He was from the 80th Infantry Division. He lay there, still, bleeding from the wound in his neck inflicted by the bayonet of a German soldier. We moved again, but only a short distance. This time my half-track came to a halt in front of a barn, where two American soldiers from the 80th Infantry Division held a group of German soldiers at bay with machine guns.

A lieutenant stepped out of the barn and motioned to one of his men, who proceeded to jab one of the Germans in the rib with the grease gun and herded him into the barn. One shot was heard. Then the lieutenant came back out of the barn and motioned for another German to be brought in. Another shot was heard, then another, until all the prisoners had been stacked like cordwood in the barn located in the still quiet village in Alsace Lorraine.

The column started moving again and reached the opposite side of the village without resistance. The Germans had left a spanking new medium tank sitting squarely in the center of the main street of the village and hauled ass. We learned that the tank had run out of gas and the crew had abandoned it to the advancing American armor.

When we reached the open country beyond the village, the

Chapter 7. God Takes Care of Drunks and Fools

Major General Manton Eddy (left) and Major General John S. Wood. Maj. Gen. Wood reported to Eddy, who was the commanding general of XII Corps (U.S. Army photograph).

driver maneuvered our vehicle into a wing on the left side of the wedge and started rolling across the open field, firing into a clump of trees that stood about two hundred feet to our left wing. The Germans had set up a machine gun nest in the woods, and as we cut across the field, they very foolishly opened fire on us.

The bullets could not penetrate the heavy armor of the half-tracks and only served to harass us. True, at first they pinned us down inside the tracks with their fire, but this lasted only long enough for us to take the initiative. I reached my hand up and grabbed the pistol grip of the .30 caliber machine gun mounted on the left side of the track and squeezed the trigger. The gun bucked in its mounting, sending a stream of fire into the woods.

When I felt I had them pinned down, I raised up behind the gun and traversed the fire, raking the entire wooded area. One of the Krauts got the same idea, for as we rolled across the open field, a stream of lead raked the side of the track, sending up a cloud of smoke and dust to tell me he was hitting his mark. All of a sudden, the track stopped smack in the middle of the field, leaving us exposed to the pleasure of the Kraut gunner.

I called out to Gross, our driver, "What in the hell are you stopping here for, Gross?"[5]

"I'm hit," he called back.

I leaned over the partition separating him from the squad seats in the rear. He was holding his left thigh. A small piece of lead from the Kraut machine gun had found its way through a small portal at his left shoulder and lodged in his leg.

I was mad as a bastard at a family reunion. "You son-of-a-bitch! If you don't get this goddamn track moving, you're gonna be

The driver compartment of the M3A1 half-track. Armored shields could be positioned over the front windshield and sides of the cabin, though the narrow observation slits limited visibility. The communications equipment in this restored vehicle is from the modern era to ensure seamless communication while in operation during reenactments (photograph by Don M. Fox).

Chapter 7. God Takes Care of Drunks and Fools

hurting a hell of a lot worse than you are now. Now get the hell out of here!"

He managed to muster what little sense he had and slammed through the gear box until we passed the danger of the woods. Upon inspecting the truck, we found they had raked its entire side. We were carrying 13 mines on either side and the bullets had drilled holes in the entire line. I don't fully understand the operation of T.N.T. but apparently these landmines needed something stronger to detonate them. Merci, mon ami.

A few days after this action, we were sent on another outpost to guard a road that afforded the German Army a means of supplying their troops. My squad had taken up a position just off the road, while one of the tanks occupied a position squarely in the middle of the road. The cannon was zeroed straight down the middle of the road and we were dug in on either side as precaution against any German infantry that might approach the tank at night.

We had only been there a short time, when a small civilian auto came hurtling down the road, about 500 yards in front of us. We waited for the car to come within 200 yards of us and opened up on the vehicle with the machine guns we had dug in beside the tank. The first burst of fire sent the vehicle plunging into a ditch, its occupants discouraged and now running across the road, hightailing it over a hell of a barren hill; no trees or foliage of any sort that might have

An infantryman mans a .30 caliber Browning M1919A4 light machine gun within a prepared position (U.S. Army photograph).

offered them protection. We continued to fire at them for three or four minutes, then took off, running down the road in the direction of the ditched auto.

One German officer was lying dead in the ditch in front of the car, while three others had made it from the hill to the rear. We took after them, but after chasing them for three, maybe four hundred yards, we lost sight of them and returned to the tank in the middle of the road.

The next morning, we mounted up and joined a task force that had been ordered to occupy the city of Lunéville in Alsace Lorraine.[6] It was a railroad division city and from what we could discern the railroad split the city pretty much in the middle. We sat on the outskirts and blasted the town for some time with heavy artillery. Then our tanks led us into town. There was no real resistance to speak of and we occupied half the town without bloodshed. Our guess had been correct. The railroad did split the town down the middle. We positioned our tanks and half-tracks along the railroad, while the German troops held to the opposite side of the tracks.

My particular half-track took up a position in the front yard of a house of considerable size and my squad began to look over the immediate surroundings, exercising every precaution, as we were not sure where the Germans were located. Within a few minutes, we spotted them dug in on the opposite side of the railroad embankment, just fifty yards from our position.

Sergeant Brown, the mortar squad leader, and I took a telephone and a roll of wire.[7] We unrolled the wire as we walked to our intended spotting station at the corner of the yard. It boasted a four-foot stone fence, which formed a wall of protection on two sides, and maximum concealment from above, as there was a tree, standing in the very corner of the yard, which hung heavy with drooping vines.

Brown and I sat in the corner of the yard and watched a squad of our men who had taken up a position on the second floor of the house next door. They had been firing down on the German troops. When they had ceased to fire, the German squad leader gave orders to his men to load their rifles with rifle grenades and fire. The grenades were aimed at the position of the American soldiers behind the

Chapter 7. God Takes Care of Drunks and Fools

M4 medium tanks on a street in Lunéville (U.S. Army photograph).

second-floor window, from which they had caused such trouble for the Germans.

We located ten German troops dug in, just across from us. Sergeant Brown gave Kovacs, his first gunner, the coordinates and instructed him to give one shot. The first round went over the Germans' position and landed about 300 yards to their rear. He gave Kovacs a correction in the coordinates and the burst from the exploding 60-millimeter mortar could be seen clearly in line with the enemy's slit trenches but 75 yards to the right. Sergeant Brown gave Kovacs another correction and told him to traverse his fire. The explosions from the mortar shells walked the full length of the line of slit trenches in front of us, then started the return trip to our left. Three times Kovacs raked the line of slit trenches before us. Then Brown instructed him to cease fire. The soldiers across the tracks quickly jumped out of their trenches and scaled a six-foot wall and all we could see was Kraut shirttails flapping in the breeze.

Sergeant Brown had first called Battalion Artillery and gave them coordinates, hoping to knock out the two tanks. But the armor piercing projectiles had too much of a flat trajectory for him to shorten the range enough to get in so close. The buildings behind us were too tall, and Brown knew that if he shortened the range and brought the fire in just across the tracks, there was a good chance of hitting one of the buildings behind us. When Sergeant Brown decided the artillery would not work, he called Kovacs, his first mortar man.

The two tanks could not be damaged or knocked out with the mortar. So, we waited and sweated them out until nightfall. About an hour after the sun went down, while twilight was still hanging over the city of Lunéville, I took two bazooka teams and scaled the wall that separated us from the tanks and took up a position behind a tree, just to the rear and center of the bazooka teams.

The tanks were just beyond the wall the German troops had scaled when Kovacs ceased fire. One of them was sitting at the approach of a viaduct which crossed the railroad tracks. We could see the tank very clearly, and I gave orders for both bazooka teams to fire at the one tank at the viaduct approach. The other was hidden behind a house and could not be seen from where we stood.

John Rice, the squad comedian, was on one of the bazookas and Dutch Wanosik held the other to his shoulder, fully loaded and ready to fire. The missile from Dutch's bazooka fishtailed across the tracks and hit the tank on the rounded part of the turret, bouncing harmlessly off, doing no damage.

John's finger pressed back on the trigger, but nothing happened. He pulled the big tube back off the top of the fence and looked at it for a second. Then, without turning around, he threw the whole shebang over the fence and hightailed it in the direction of the fence we had to scale to avoid the line of fire we were sure would come. The flash from the bazooka gave away our position, and we had scarcely scaled the fence when the machine guns from across the tracks sent a hail of fire into the yard. Still can't understand why they didn't set down on the trigger of the "88" mounted on their tank, but I suppose it is not wise to look a gift horse in the mouth. We were just fortunate they didn't. *Merci, mon ami.*

War is indeed strange, and interesting things happen in war. Before Brown came to the corner of the yard with the telephone, I had been lying there, looking over the fence, with my eyes raised just far enough to see the action in the trenches without exposing too much of my head. I was completely wrapped up in what I was

Chapter 7. God Takes Care of Drunks and Fools

watching as four Free French of the Interior men came strolling down the sidewalk. They came upon me so quickly and walked so close to my position that they caught me completely off guard and scared the hell out of me. Realizing who they were, I didn't move. I didn't want them stopping to talk with me, for this would give away my position. They had not seen the German troops dug in across the tracks, to whom they were completely exposed. The German soldiers, however, offered them no resistance, and they went their way, completely oblivious to what the war was all about. True to the old saying, "God takes care of drunks and fools."

My half-track driver had been standing in the yard, talking to the driver of another half-track, when Kovacs had started dropping the rounds of mortar into the tube. They were still in conversation when one of the fins came off a mortar shell. Instead of dropping on the German troops across the track, it had found its way to the ground between the half-track drivers but failed to explode. The men were standing only three feet apart, when the shell hit the ground directly between them. Needless to say, the dud broke off the conversation, as they hightailed it in two different directions. The shell never exploded. Strange.

CHAPTER 8

THE MYSTERIES OF WAR

We left the city of Lunéville and drew back ten miles. The 6th Armored Division passed through us to occupy the city. When we were sure the division had taken over our former positions, our command left the area. Within a few days, we took up a running battle with a German *Panzer* division around the city of Nancy in Alsace Lorraine. Our tanks and tank destroyers left 26 of the enemy tanks on the field, completely demobilized, then left the area to take up a position 25 miles east of the city of Nancy, where we dug in and were to remain for 26 days.[1]

We dug in on the side of a hill overlooking the city of Moyenvic and the first two days we looked the area over.[2] When we were fully determined there were no German troops in the area, we walked down the side of a hill and took up a position in a sheep herder's trailer, where four of us played pinochle for two days. At first, we played cutthroat, and although I kept them busy watching me when it came my time to deal, I still lost what little money I had. I managed to slip a double pinochle on the bottom of the deck each time I dealt, but when I consistently kept coming down with it in my meld, I was barred from the game.

I busied myself with taking the door off the trailer. Growing tired of this, I returned to the hillside, where we had dug our trenches. We had spent the days in the trailer and at night we would return to our trenches to sleep. I took the trailer door with me and laid it over the 2-by-6–foot trench I had dug, then spread a good twenty inches of earth on top of the door, which offered me greater protection from the aerial bursts that were to come later that first week.

Chapter 8. The Mysteries of War

On the fifth day the Germans moved in three tanks across the valley and busied themselves with direct fire from the "88's." This broke up our pinochle game. The gunners were so quick and accurate with their action that we dared not stick our heads too far out of the trenches during the day. All through the day we awaited the return fire of our tanks which had taken up a position 300 to 400 yards to our rear. Six of our tanks, with howitzer cannons mounted on them, stood their ground. For the better part of three weeks, both day and night, they exchanged a deadly fire with the German tanks across the valley. They reduced the town of Moyenvic to rubble.

Then one day, as we sat in our trenches, looking across the valley, a battalion of German troops came across the open fields, marching abreast to form a line laterally and across the entire width of the open fields. Our platoon leaders sent down an order for us to hold our fire, as they wanted the German troops to approach within a hundred yards. We were not to fire before then.

Had this order been obeyed, there would have been no opportunity of escape for the Krauts, but when their line approached to a distance within five hundred yards of our position, and kept coming closer, an Indian boy from the Blackfoot tribe just couldn't stand the pressure. He opened up on them with an M1 and emptied a clip of .30 caliber into their midst. When this happened, our entire line opened fire on the approaching enemy.

The German troops in the valley below were at an extreme disadvantage. When our line opened fire on them, they were compelled to hit the ground and wait for their tanks, which were moving about on the opposite hillside, to take the initiative for them. I was first gunner on a .30 caliber machine gun at the time and had two or three boxes of ammunition for the air-cooled machine in the hole with me.

Dutch Wanosik was on a .50 caliber gun he had mounted from the turret of the track, and between us we were laying down approximately 600 rounds of red-hot lead per minute in the direction of the line before us.

The tracers appeared to be forming an upward crescent, or a saucer-like trail, as they left the mouths of the bucking guns to fall on the enemy, lying face down on the ground of the valley below us.

The .50 caliber M2 machine gun was mounted on a ring which allowed it to traverse 360 degrees. The M2 was used against ground targets and aircraft (photograph by Don M. Fox).

I very quickly ran out of ammunition and jumped out of the trench. I ran back to the half-track to replace it. I honestly believe that had I not run out of ammunition, I would have melted the barrel of the gun, for I could not prevent myself from hanging on the trigger, as I traversed the line of troops before me. It was like I was shooting ducks on a mill pond.

I raced over the hill and jumped to the rear of the half-track, grabbing a case of ammunition. I leaped back to the ground and headed in a dead run to the front line. I didn't want to miss any of the sport while the ducks were still on the pond. As I raced along the open field of the crest of the hillside, three or four tanks came up in back of me, heading over the hill in the direction of the German troops. The German tanks spotted our tanks coming over the hill and opened fire. Our tanks began zigzagging across the top of the hill, as the fire kept coming down in their midst.

I was caught in the open field and could hear the shrapnel bouncing off our tanks, causing me no little amount of alarm. I gave

Chapter 8. The Mysteries of War

The rear entry to the half-track. Ammunition storage was in the forward section of the seating area (photograph by Don M. Fox).

up the attempt and dropped the case of ammunition and headed for a ravine a hundred yards to my left.

Our tanks moved on over the side of the hill, as the German tanks pulled their fire down on the line of our infantry. The tanks were momentarily halted behind a clump of trees just to the rear of our line and the German tanks could not see them well enough to direct their fire. This allowed me to leap to my feet and run to the top of the hill, where I had left the ammunition when the tanks approached. I reached down to take hold of the case of ammunition. It was then that I discovered I had been carrying .50 caliber ammunition instead of the .30 caliber ammunition my machine gun required. I ran back to the half-track, secured a case of .30 caliber ammunition, and then ran back to the trench, where I had left the red-hot machine gun.

As I raced over the top of the hill, I passed the trench of a second lieutenant who had been field commissioned from the rank of tech sergeant.[3] He was frozen in the bottom of the trench he had dug a few days previously. This man had landed with the company back in Normandy and had been hit in the back with a small piece of shrapnel during the first battle of the hedgerows, where we were all baptized. They sent him to a hospital back in England. Later, he was returned to our outfit as a lieutenant. Back in Normandy he did not see the first Kraut, but was hit by a piece of shrapnel. He had been lying on his hump in a comfortable bed with sheets back in bloody England, and now they saw fit to spot commission him because he had been such a good spit and polish man back in the States. Goddamnit to hell! Those officers in the company bracket didn't know their asses from a hole in the ground, or they would never have commissioned this dog.

As I passed his trench, he was crying like a kid with his ass spanked. "What's the matter with you, Greenockle," I asked him, looking down at him crying in the bottom of the hole. I don't remember what he said in reply, but to the best of my knowledge he said nothing, for he seemed too afraid to speak.[4]

Our tanks had stopped behind a small clump of trees just to the rear of our trenches, and as I passed one of them, its commander asked me if we had any mines in the field in front of us. I answered in the affirmative. He asked me to get another man or two and take them up so the tanks could get through the hole to the German troops down in the valley. I grabbed two men from the line. We ran down the side of the hill, grabbing eight or ten of the mines off the top of the ground and returned to the trenches. We had laid the mines on top of the ground, as we were only interested in guarding against a night approach by any of the German tanks that may have cared to venture in our direction.

Our three tanks proceeded through the opening we provided for them and lumbered down the hillside in the direction of the German troops who were still pinned to the valley floor below us. The tanks moved so slowly and were so very much out in the open that it made me nervous to watch them move to their destruction. I now know why, but I did not then know why the German tanks waited on the opposite hill for our tanks to reach the bottom of the valley.

They had waited until our tanks were in a position of no return and then opened fire on them. Each time a German gunner touched

Chapter 8. The Mysteries of War

the trigger on an "88," a piece of one of our tanks would dislodge itself from the vehicle of which it was part and fly through the air, landing fifty or so yards away. The first shot hit the lead tank and the track flew fifty feet into the air. The crew jumped out of the tank and headed hell bent for election for a clump of trees a hundred yards away.

The second shot dismounted the turret from another of the tanks, but I don't remember seeing any of the crew leave the wounded monster.

The third tank, with his latches buttoned down, could not see what had happened to his comrades, and continued towards the German troops before him. When he reached them, five of them leaped from the ground and sprang to the back of the tank. I very quickly turned my machine gun in the direction of the tank and pulled back on the trigger. At the same time, I called to Dutch, who was on the .50 caliber, to turn his gun on the tank. The combined fire of the 30 and .50 caliber guns knocked the Krauts off the back of the tank, and its commander realized something was amiss. He ordered his driver to turn the tank around, which he did very quickly, and started back up the side of the hill.

Our anti-tank platoon had a 57-millimeter cannon dug in just thirty feet behind us. They had spotted the positions of the German tanks that had been giving our tanks so much hell. The 57 behind us coughed a few times, then there was silence on the opposite hillside. Our one remaining tank made it through the field of mines and disappeared over the hill behind us. The German tanks had relocated and turned their fire once again on the demobilized tanks in the valley.

That night our platoon lieutenant came to my trench with a sergeant by the name of Strong. They asked me to accompany them on a mission to demobilize the 76-millimeter cannon that was mounted on one of our crippled medium tanks down in the valley. They told me they were afraid the German infantry might get in the tank and turn the cannon on us. If this were to happen, they would knock the hell out of us at such close range. I crawled down the hill with them.

When we reached the bottom of the hillside, I suddenly found myself in the lead position, but didn't think anything of it at the time. I was out on a point, with the lieutenant to my right and rear some twenty-five feet. Sergeant Strong was to my left and rear the same distance. He and the lieutenant had fallen behind as we walked to the demobilized tanks. I got close enough to the tanks to distinguish their outline, but this was as close as I could get. There was a sudden burst of machine gun fire, which cut through the air over my head, and I hit the ground. I lay there for a thirty second period, not saying anything, nor did I move. I was trying to find out where the fire was coming from. The lieutenant called out to me, "Hey, Porter, what you gonna do?"

I turned my head in the direction of his voice and replied, "I don't know what you're gonna do, but I'm getting the hell out of here!"

Before I finished the statement I was on my feet, running past him and Sergeant Strong, heading for the hillside and the safety of the darkness. The Krauts had obviously dismounted one of the .30 caliber machine guns from one of our tanks and had turned the damned thing on us as we approached. I was, at any rate, not going to force the issue. I was out in the open field and damn sure didn't want to make a dead hero of myself by approaching them in the dark. I melted into the darkness.

I still don't know how long Lieutenant Green and Sergeant Strong remained out there before they got the message. I didn't hear any more of the machine gun chatter, or any loud explosions from the phosphorus grenades they were supposed to have slid down the mouth of the 76-millimeter cannon, so I just assumed they followed my admonition and got the hell out of there.

During the time of our stay on the hillside, my second gunner, Blackie, grew very apprehensive at the thought of returning to the safety of the States. He bugged me day and night to shoot him in the leg. Blackie felt that he only had a one-way ticket on the steamer that brought us to France, and as the days grew into weeks and the artillery continued to fall around us, he almost got out of hand, yearning to get off the line. One day I crawled out of the trench and ran a few feet to the rear to talk with Dutch. While I was gone, an artillery shell landed approximately three feet from the hole that housed

Chapter 8. The Mysteries of War

Blackie. The shell ripped out a hole about a foot deep and two feet wide, sending shrapnel through the ammunition box alongside the machine gun we had mounted on a tripod beside the hole.

Shrapnel had knocked the hell out of the gun but it was still in working order. When I got back to the hole, Blackie was beside himself and said, "Goddamnit Porter. If you had shot me in the leg, I would have been somewhere safe, sleeping in a comfortable bed."

A week previously he had bugged me so hard to shoot him that I laid the plan. I told him I would go out of the hole and run to the rear of the trees that clumped a few feet behind us. I instructed him to tell anybody that asked that I had gone to the crapper. When I came back to the trench, he was to have his leg held up and away from his body. I would shoot him and make it look like a sniper had hit him while he was coming back to the hole, and I would tell the story that it had been me not Blackie who had gone to the crapper with the plan well in mind.

I had crawled out of the trench and ran behind the clump of trees, where I remained for a short time. When I ran back down the side of the hill and dropped off into the trench, Blackie had his leg held high in the air. He was trembling and his face was almost white, when I drew down on his leg and pulled the trigger. The bullet was deliberately aimed to miss him, and when the shot was fired, Blackie's leg was trembling so hard that I couldn't help but break into a laugh. I tried to pull him out of his state of depression, but to no avail.

Now, Blackie was goading me again to shoot him. I told him, "Hold your goddamn leg up."

I jumped out of the trench and ran back to the clump of trees. I waited for just a few seconds and ran back to the hole. As I dropped into the hole, Blackie was ready and waiting. I raised the German pistol I had been carrying in my hip packet and holding the muzzle about four inches from his leg, I pulled the trigger. The gun bucked in my hand and Blackie jerked his leg away from the mouth of the trench as if he had been hit with a jolt of electricity. I took my trench knife and ripped the leg of his trousers, pulling the thick material over his knee to expose a small round hole that had been bored in the calf of his leg. Much to my surprise, the hole had sealed itself on both sides of the leg and wasn't even bleeding. Fortunately, I had missed the bone and any major blood vessels, but I began to worry about the black powder burns around the wound. There was a round spot about the size of a silver dollar around the wound. I spit on his leg and tried to wipe it off, but it would not come off. Then I took a handful of dirt and mixed it with the spit, rubbing the hell out of the round spot, but it still would not come off. The powder burn was there to stay, and I knew Blackie would catch hell when the doctor reported his findings to the provost marshal's office.

Somebody down the line called, "What happened, Porter?"

"A sniper shot Blackie in the leg!"

Our platoon lieutenant immediately got the heavy weapons on the platoon telephone and gave them orders to lay a barrage in the valley below our positions. The 81-millimeter mortar shells began whistling over our heads and bursting below us. The mortar man began traversing his fire to rake the entire length of the valley, but I don't believe there was anything out there other than two or three stray cows, grazing as if there were no such thing as war! He laid down about 25 rounds before the lieutenant gave an order to cease fire, and two or three cows lay very dead in the valley below us.

A jeep came buzzing over the hill to stop a few feet from the trench, where Blackie and I had been shacked up for better than three weeks. The medics had Blackie on the stretcher in no time, and one of them was busy pouring sulfa drugs on the wound. As they picked him up to put him on the back of the jeep, he looked up at me, and winking in a gesture of friendship, said "Thanks, Porter."

The jeep shot over the hill and that was the last I saw of Blackie. But he left me something to remember him by, for before I shot him, I made him promise to give me his Smith and Wesson .44, an accordion he had looted from some Frenchman's house, and 17 dollars in cash.

One day as we sat there on the side of the hill, the Kraut artillery started beating the hell out of our positions. Joe Kiernan, the rifleman, who had been taken prisoner back at Avranches, crawled out of his hole and started walking up and down the line. He seemed to be

Chapter 8. The Mysteries of War

in a deep state of confusion, rubbing his face and wringing his hands as he walked to and fro along the line. It had been raining like hell for two days, and the artillery coupled with the pounding rain was just too much for Joe's mind. He had snapped and was completely oblivious to the danger around him.

The artillery shells were exploding along the entire line, but Joe just kept walking back and forth. I don't remember who ran out in the streaming shrapnel to get him, nor do I remember whether or not he made it to his trench alone. All I do remember is that when I saw him walking up and down the line during an artillery barrage, raining water and steel, I was preoccupied with staying alive and dared not raise out of the trench which felt as safe as Fort Knox. Might have been chicken, but I am alive, if that is any accomplishment.

There is a mystery in war. Many things happen in war that are not explainable. I say this because of one particular thing that happened while we sat on that hillside, exchanging small arms and artillery fire with the enemy. The first four days there was no enemy at all in the area. All we did was play pinochle and dig holes in the ground. Then the anti-tank platoon moved a half-track that had a 57-millimeter cannon into its position just 20 feet behind the trenches we'd dug. The cannon was dismounted and set into a position to command a field of fire that covered the entire valley below us.

For 22 days that half-track sat back there, a clump of small trees its only protection, while artillery shells dug huge holes in the ground all around the vehicle. It would be safe to estimate that the enemy artillery and tanks dropped a minimum of a thousand rounds of exploding steel heads around the half-track, and not one of those projectiles hit the track. When the order came down for us to move out of that position, we inspected the track and were amazed at the number of shrapnel marks found on the sides of the vehicle. The half-track just wasn't in the pot.

Another arcanum that will always be a mystery to me is the incident of Joe Kiernan crawling out of his trench to walk up and down the line of holes, while the enemy was traversing our line with a deadly hall of exploding shells. Why didn't that man get hit? He just wasn't in the pot.

You're a Good Man, Sergeant

Still another mystery is the order that came down from Division, halting our command on that particular hill. That first four days there was no enemy present. The terrain was open and free of claim. Why did we not move on and take it? Our objective had been known for some time, and when it was there for the taking, we were ordered to halt. Back in Troyes, a good hundred plus miles to the rear, we had been told that our objective was Strasbourg on the Rhine. When we moved into position on the side of the hill overlooking the village of Moyenvic, Alsace Lorraine, we were in trim, spoiling for a fight. Instead of moving the fight to the enemy we waited for 26 days to take a hell of a drubbing with artillery and sporadic small arms fighting.

At last, the 26th Division was moved under cover of darkness to take over our positions. When they arrived, each machine gun, rifle, and mortar squad exchanged positions with them, and they were informed as to what they were confronted with. The squad leader of the machine gun section was directed to my trench. I crawled out of the hole to greet him and to warn him of his plight. As the two of us stood beside the trench talking, his men waited in the background to be told which position to take. To get you to the valley a vehicle roared into action, moving a hundred feet and stopping.

The next thing that came to our attention was the monstrous sound of a projectile. It sounded as if it were being directed under tremendous force of pressure through the barrel of a gun too small to accommodate the missile. We directed our sight to a trail of fire that swept across the darkness, arching through the sky and looking for our position. While the Screaming Meemie thundered through the sky, looking for something to destroy, I turned, and with one swift movement, dove into the trench beside me. The sound was not at all familiar to my ear and it terrorized me to the bone.

It had happened so quickly that the man from the 26th Infantry Division was, I am sure, caught off guard, for he was still standing beside the trench when the Screaming Meemie struck the ground and exploded. The projectile had landed 50 feet to the right of my position, tearing a hole in the ground three feet wide and 18 inches

Chapter 8. The Mysteries of War

deep. It left a burnt circle, 25 feet in diameter, around the hole it had dug. This was the first of the eerie sounding vehicles of destruction that had been sent in our direction, and although we were familiar with the various sounds of war, we were struck with terror by this screaming noise. It was directed upon us as a demoralizing agent. It had served its purpose well.

The 26th Infantry Division had just arrived from the States. They were green as gourds to the laws that governed war and its action. We bid them adieu, and, taking our weapons on our humps, slid over the hill to leave them to whatever fate held in store for them.

We climbed aboard our half-tracks and joined the column that had formed on the road a few hundred yards away. We stopped stock still for God only knows what. That goddamn army had a way of just pissing a man off. They'd hurry like hell to get you off the line of fire and out of danger, then pull you back a few yards from the front line and stop the damned column. We had aroused the German troops below by cranking up all those goddamn engines and they knew we were preparing to either move out or attack. They didn't know which, but either way, they weren't going to just sit there like a bump on a log waiting for us. They opened up with a hell of an artillery barrage, but we were fortunate enough to bear the brunt of the attack.

Goddamn the son-of-a-bitch who stopped the column of half-tracks. We lay out on the opposite side of the hill for a good ten minutes, while the Krauts beat the hell out of us with their famous "88's." Couldn't do a damn thing about it until some son-of-a-bitch up front made up his mind which crossroad to take. Why in the hell didn't he make up his goddamn mind before he mounted us up and we cranked up all those friggin engines? It caused the Kraut's artillery to spot our positions. SNAFU'D again![5]

We were held in reserve until the commander of the combat command we were attached to was sure the 26th Infantry Division was going to hold our former positions. We sure were glad to move away from that friggin hill. Bless God, the bastard finally made up his mind which road to take! We hauled ass to the rear about five miles and bivouacked in an open field for the night. We sat there for three days and mounted up again. We moved further back to a location just outside the city of Nancy in Alsace Lorraine, where we were to remain for another two days.

Chapter 9

A New Buck Sergeant

On the first day, we were herded into six-by-sixes like swine and taken into the city of Nancy, where we were to take a bath. It was the first soap and water we had seen for better than two months. We pulled up to the municipal swimming pool and dismounted to hurry into the water that looked so inviting. We showered and hit the pool like a bunch of school kids, but I for one was not satisfied with so small a bone. By God, I wanted something I was damn certain the officers of our company were going to get. I wanted to get dog drunk and go looking for the sporting girls.[1]

Sergeant Keyes and I slipped out of the water and got dressed. We very quietly walked away from the rest of the men, who were climbing back into the six-by-six for the return trip to the company area. We had walked only two or three blocks when we were accosted by two military policemen, who shouted to us in the dark, "Halt there! You two fellows hold up!"

In reply, I yelled back to them, "You go to hell, you bastards! We'll see you in about ten years." With this, we broke into a sprint that carried us into the darkness, where we disappeared.

The M.P.s chased us for a short distance, and when they saw we were going to outdistance them in the dark, they ceased their chase and the two of us headed for the red-light district. It wasn't at all difficult to find the section that had bugged us, for all we had to do was follow the stream of drunken G.I.s, who were returning from the Avenue of Mademoiselles. They were returning to their motor pools, and we needed only to follow in reverse the trail they made.

About the only thing I remember of that night's action was the room we finally folded up in. I remember hearing the distant cannon, as they thundered their old familiar theme of death and destruction, distant rumbles of cannon echoing through the open window to remind us that there was still a war going on.

We fell, finally, from the pinnacle of consciousness into an exhausted slumber to awake in the early morning hours and get after it. We dressed, went downstairs, and looked the situation over to see if there were any M.P.s in the area. When we were satisfied there were none, we hauled freight. Naturally, the first stop we made was in a wine shop, where we fortified ourselves for the day's coming action. At about nine that morning, we meandered into the section we had been looking for the night before and settled down to some serious drinking.

The red-light district covered both sides of the street for four blocks, where it ended, then went in either direction for another three blocks. The street was literally jammed to the gunwales with G.I.s, most of whom were as drunk as a baron on cognac, beer, wine, and blood. We finally set up our operation in a small house of ill repute, where not too many G.I.s congregated, and for the better part of two hours things went well. We stood at the end of the bar and tried to forget the 26 days we'd spent on the side of the hill that overlooked Moyenvic.

A small blonde waited on us from behind the bar. All she had on her trim little blonde body was a pair of sheer panties and a brassiere, which barely covered her. I had been standing at the end of the bar, as the day progressed. Each time she came to the end of the bar to wait on us, I reached behind her and pinched her very lightly on the rump. She didn't seem to take exception, but an M.P. who had entered the bar and taken a position beside me at the rail, grew very apprehensive every time I patted the good-looking girl on the rump.

I reached out to pat her on the rump again and the M.P. grabbed a hand full of my hair and twisted me to the floor. My carbine was zipped in its cover, leaning against the bar. I reached over, took the zipper catch between my fingers, and ripped the cover off the weapon. Then I grabbed the small rifle out of the cover and jammed it in the MP's belly, saying, "Let go, you son-of-a-bitch or I'll blow your goddamn guts out!"

Chapter 9. A New Buck Sergeant

He dropped me like a hot potato, and I raised myself to the bar again. I jabbed the M.P. in the gut with the barrel of the gun again and told him to get the hell out of the joint. He didn't confuse the issue and walked very hastily to the street and disappeared. Keyes and I stayed just long enough to make a graceful exit, for we knew the M.P. left to get one of his asshole buddies and would return. We had no authority to be in town and knew they would rawhide us if they got us over a barrel.

We walked one block to another swinging cathouse and bucked the line that had formed outside on the street. There must have been fifty G.I.s lined up like Christmas candy on the street outside the cathouse, but we went straight to the door and walked in. The madam of the house told us very quickly, "You two are drunk. Go walk around for a while, then come back."

We left and did just that. Within an hour, we were back, bucking the line again, and this time, the madam gave us each a girl. We disappeared upstairs.

I didn't last long, as I had not been in the company of a woman in more than two months. The girl jumped out of bed and slipped on her pants, which is all she wore, and ran quickly out of the room because she wanted to get another G.I. upstairs as quickly as possible. Three hundred francs a pop and her bottom drawer was half full of hundred-franc notes.

I sat on the side of the bed for just an instant, things not seeming right, and thought of the quicky she had tossed me. I jumped to my feet, holding a small Italian pistol in my fist. I leaped to the door, stepped out onto the landing and pointed the pistol down the stairwell. "Mademoiselle! Viene ce!"

She halted at the bottom of the staircase and looked at me, with some concern registered on her face. She was not sure whether or not I would use the pistol, so she didn't argue the point. She mounted the steps and very quickly entered the room. I sat on the bed and casually laced my boots, as she stood waiting, patiently. I went downstairs and got Keyes and we left. The quick mademoiselle was a step closer to understanding than before.

Having blown all our dough, we headed back to the swimming

pool, hoping there would be a truck from the company waiting for us. There had only been about twenty of us brought from the outfit on the previous day and we were sure that another truckload would be brought in to take a bath. As we walked back toward the swimming pool, we passed a captain, who was all decked out in his O.D.s, complete with tie and everything. The good captain walked on the opposite side of the street and called out, "Don't you soldiers know how to salute in your outfit?" We stopped.

"Why, yes sir, captain," I retorted, with more than average cynicism registered in my voice. Then I swayed back until I was looking straight into the sky, and raising my hand with the palm facing him, let it drift to the ground like a falling leaf. Without stopping to think the situation over, Keyes and I tore off down the street, and as we passed the good captain's position I called to him, "I'll see you in about ten years, you gourd-headed bastard!"

Spit and polish son-of-a bitch from OCS, who thought there was nothing more to war than saluting a no-good bastard who had never laid his eyes on a Kraut.[2]

It was still early in the afternoon, and we didn't expect the truck to leave the city until six in the evening. So, I told Keyes we would make it to one of the best restaurants in the city and hang the rigging on them for something to eat. He agreed and we went into one of the finer places to sample their culinary art. As we sat down at the table, I looked around at the crowd, which had gathered for the afternoon repast, and told Keyes to leave his helmet on his head and his rifle swung over his shoulder. I had made up my mind that we were going to eat and drink our fill and then just get up and walk out. If they stopped us, I was prepared to tell them thanks and just continue walking.

We ordered the finest on the menu and had the waiter bring us a jug of wine. By the time he arrived with the food order, we were out of wine and ordered another jug. We ate and finished off another jug. I informed Keyes that I was going to get up from the table and walk through the archway which led to the bar. He agreed to follow at a reasonable interval, and I stepped through the archway. I turned, but Keyes was still at the table, hesitating to rise and walk out.

Chapter 9. A New Buck Sergeant

As I stood in the archway, looking at him, it suddenly struck me to galvanize him into action. I slipped my two little fingers up to my lips, and curving my tongue into an areola, I let out a blast of air that formed into a shrill whistle. "Keyes, you son-of-a-bitch, come on! Let's get the hell out of here!"

He suddenly jumped to his feet and ran past me through the archway. We hit the revolving door with a bang. The door swung like a whirling dervish and Keyes was on the street running. I ran to the door and entered the whirling circle. I was literally tossed to the sidewalk, falling on my face. The door had thrown me. I scrambled to my feet and tore after Keyes, who was flat laying her down, Sam.

We made it back to the company area without incident and nothing was said of our absence. Keyes went back to take command of his squad and I melted very quietly back to mine. Nobody said anything and I kept quiet.

The next day, as we sat in the bivouac area, Keyes came over to my half-track and asked me if I had anything to drink. He had a bad case of the whips and jingles and wanted something to quiet him down. I had a full case of cognac in the track but hesitated to break it out. Instead, I gave him a bottle of very sweet liqueur and he broke into it like he didn't give a damn what it was.

After an hour of steady drinking, he was drunk again and I slipped a fireman's hold on him, and throwing him over my shoulder, I started back to his half-track. On the way I passed the company commander. He was sitting on a ration case beside his half-track. He looked at us but didn't say anything. I deposited Keyes and returned to my squad. Man! That fella Keyes sure did take his juice. He had been poisoned twice since his arrival in France. The Krauts had a nasty habit of poisoning wine before they left an area, and Keyes just couldn't keep his snoot out of the jug.

While we sat there, just waiting to make certain that the 26th Division was going to hold our former positions, we busied ourselves by cleaning our weapons and gear. I spent most of my time shooting the breeze with the cooks. One day, as I sat in the cook tent, word came to me that Sergeant Strong, second in command of the machine gun squad, had shot himself in the thigh while he was cleaning a German Luger. Seems as though he had the clip in the weapon, with the breech pulled back, cleaning the chamber. His hand slipped, allowing the barrel to fall back into a closed position. Evidently, he had his finger wrapped around the trigger, and when the barrel slid home, the gun bucked and spit a round of angry steel through his leg.[3]

I hadn't particularly liked or disliked Strong. He was a very quiet man, who never did anything but follow the orders which came down to him through channels. He had been a Pfc. for as long as I had known him, and I didn't particularly like a goddamn Pfc. Seemed to me that a man who would allow himself to be bought for an extra dollar a month couldn't be too much. I had stayed away from Strong as much as possible. So, as I sat there in the kitchen tent, shooting up my experiences with the cooks, who hadn't seen much action, the information that Sergeant Strong had shot himself didn't move me one way or the other.

Strong had made buck sergeant when Sgt. Boeck had been hit and I didn't like this action worth a goddamn. He had never done anything to earn the position, for he had never taken it upon himself to exercise any initiative whatsoever. When volunteers were asked to do anything that wasn't in the line of duty, he always said no and stayed back and sat on his rump, while those who mingled freely with the other men did what was necessary.

The dumb son-of-a-bitch couldn't find his ass with both hands and the company commander put him over a bunch of men who could stand flat footed and tell the shave-tailed lieutenants, who thought they were the only ones fighting the war, to go to hell. I didn't even go to tell him goodbye because I didn't feel moved to.

When I got back to my half-track, a runner walked up to me and told me the company commander wanted to see me. I saddled my ass and walked over to the company commander's track. He told me he was going to make me a buck sergeant and place me in command of the second section of my squad. Bless God, I thought to myself, this son-of-a-bitch must need me real bad to make me a buck sergeant. I didn't say anything to him. I walked back to the squad and told

Chapter 9. A New Buck Sergeant

Sergeant Dominico, who was the squad leader, that I had been picked to replace Sergeant Strong.[4]

Service-wise, Dominico was the oldest man in the squad. He had been with the division since its formation in the state of New York. He was well liked by the men, and when Sergeant Boeck was knocked out of action by the grenade back at Avranches, the company commander put another stripe on Dominico's sleeve and made him a squad leader. He had always liked me because I was the running mate of Dutch Wanosik, who was his favorite of the squad. I was the second oldest man in the squad behind Dominico and now the two of us were in command.

As I sit, writing this account, my mind wanders back to the scene and I am made to remember that perhaps it was right for Strong to have been promoted, if only for such a short time. He had earned the rank but just didn't have the spunk to lead. I say that he had earned the rank just by being on the line for such a long time. Anybody that went through so much for such a long time should be made a full colonel, if only to draw the pay.

A few days later our company was moved to a small village outside the city of Nancy, where we were given the responsibility of guarding a railroad bridge and its surrounding yards. This lasted for about four or five days, then we moved out into the immediate countryside, pulling wet runs on pillboxes and tank traps, preparatory to moving against the Siegfried line, which boasted a chain of pillboxes guarding the German frontier.[5]

My company was briefed on the tactics to be used in assaulting the pillboxes. When we were thoroughly critiqued, we were split into assault teams and made our first attack on a pillbox that had been simulated to represent the real McCoy.[6]

Each team had a man who carried a Bangalore torpedo, which was a long pipe, filled with high explosives. It had a short fuse that would detonate the charge in quick time after it had been placed under the concertina wire around the pillboxes. Also, each team carried a pole pack of T.N.T, which was designed to blow a hole in the side of the pillboxes when placed in position. The pole was about six feet long and had a ten-pound charge of explosives tied to one end.

The charge was fitted with a short fuse timed to allow the man who carried it ample opportunity to get away from the explosion, but only if he were in a dead run. It was cutting it real close.

The machine gun squad held the flanks, firing at an oblique angle into the pillboxes and holding the enemy down, while the men with the Bangalore torpedoes and pole packs carried them to their targets. A man with a fifty-pound flamethrower went before them, and it was his duty to get as close to the pillboxes as possible and send an arm of fire into the opening nearest his position. While this was being accomplished, the men with the torpedoes and pole charges were maneuvering into position and the riflemen gave supporting small arms fire to hold down the occupants of the boxes.

We moved across the open field under a blanket of heavy artillery fire, and when we reached the center of the field, our mortar men started feeding rounds into the open-mouthed tubes, sending several rounds into the air before we had time to hit the ground. All the riflemen and submachine gun men sent a constant hail of fire into the pillbox under assault, while we of the machine gun squad brought up the flanks, tightening the fire against the pillbox.

Then all hell broke loose. The fins started falling off the mortar shells, causing them to lose all sense of direction. They spilled to the ground in the middle of the field, where our company was deployed in the attack against the pillbox. The mortar men had no way of knowing what was happening, and before word could be sent back to them to hold their fire, they had exploded ten rounds of 60-millimeter fire into our midst.

I broke out of the middle of that field like a wild horse, trying to get out of the deadly shrapnel that sang a death song around my ears, and ran headlong into a barbed wire fence. I backed off and jumped through the strands of barbed wire, tearing long gashes along my thighs. I didn't feel the wire tearing through my hide because there was something more important racing through my mind: just get through that goddamn fence and get away from it all.

After the war we found that there were two brothers by the name of Gerson who had manufactured the faulty ammunition. They were investigated by a Congressional Committee and tried for their

Chapter 9. A New Buck Sergeant

neglect. Don't know what happened to them, but I suppose they were paid in kind for the ammunition that caused us all to call it a day back in the field.

We tried no more pillboxes of the dry run caliber that day, or the next. Instead, we were called back to the front, where we were supposed to try our luck on the real McCoy, the pillboxes of the Siegfried Line, which stretched before the Rhine River a few miles from the city of Strasbourg. We left the area of Nancy, and in a few days, were drawing a tight ring around the city of Château Salins, a small village commanding a crossroad that was vital to the communication system of the German armies, who were defending a line from that village to the North Sea, where the Rhine River disgorged. It began to snow and get kind of cold for outdoor living, but the line had to be extended and the crossroad had to be taken, for the Third Army was just short of making contact with the Seventh Army, which was coming up through the Belfort Gap, just south of our position.[7]

Chapter 10

Another Town to Clear

When we assaulted the Village of Château Salins, I was reminded of something General Patton had told us back in England: "When you are making an attack, men, I want every gun in your outfit to be barking death. I want every man in the company to scream like a wild Comanche. If you've got a gun that won't fire, throw the goddamn thing away and get one that will fire. I want some noise made when you are in an attack."[1]

Our tanks came up on the left of us and rolled through an apple orchard, bowling the trees over like straws. Their cannon belched periodically, rocking the tanks back on their tread, while the black smoke spilled out of their muzzles, close on the heels of the red hot steel which screamed through the air to find its mark and rain destruction and death upon the small village; destruction to their buildings and death to any who were foolish enough to remain under such a barrage.

Before we assaulted the village, our fighter planes had flown over, each of them dropping two 500-pound bombs, which literally destroyed the town-site before our tanks went in to complete the job with their cannon. When they ordered our half-tracks to move into the village, most of the damage had already been done. All we had to do was flush out the few snipers who had remained to stall us. The village was literally destroyed. Kaput, as a Kraut would say.[2]

We occupied the town and set up housekeeping in an orchard a hundred yards to the east, facing the Kraut, who had his back to the Rhine, fighting for every inch of ground between us and that mighty river.

Chapter 10. Another Town to Clear

That evening one of our half-tracks was pulling into an orchard across the way when the left front wheel struck a land mine. The front end of the vehicle jumped into the air and tilted to one side from the impact. The wheel was ripped from its mounting and hurled into the sky, while a giant puff of black smoke billowed from the ground, seemingly helping the wheel to escape the arduous task of carrying the machine it had been joined to. The impact broke the driver's legs just below the knee, and it was the end of the war for that noble driver.[3]

We remained in that position for three days, then pulled back and headed in a southerly direction, trying to make contact with the Seventh Army. Late in the evening the company pulled into a small village—I'll be damned if I can remember the name of it—and came to a dead stop in the middle of town. There was no resistance, but we were not sure that all hell wouldn't break loose at any moment.[4]

As we sat there waiting to see what the order would be, I noticed a 57-millimeter anti-tank gun parked in front of a house only a few feet from us. When we dismounted for the night, the residents of the house told us it had been left by the Germans. They had run out of ammunition and left the gun in a hurry, for they knew they probably would never use it again.

When the order came down for us to take shelter in the village houses, I took possession of the one that was nearest my half-track and had the anti-tank gun parked in its yard. As I went into the house, the owner, a man of sixty or thereabouts, came out of the basement and approached me. He was curious as to what it was I was doing in his house. I told him I was commandeering the house for myself and my soldiers, as we were very tired. I told him that he and his family would have to use the basement, as I was taking the ground floor and the upstairs rooms for my platoon. He didn't give me any guff. We took our gear off the track and hauled it into the house. By God, we set up housekeeping right there.

About 10:00 o'clock that night the Krauts started bombarding the town with a tank that was sitting just over the hill. Every now and then they would pull the tank up to the top of the hill and fire directly down into the village, with deadly accuracy, allowing no escape for their targets. As the artillery raked the town, we kept to the protection of the houses, and each time a shell fell, a murmur came up from the basement of the house where we had taken shelter.

I couldn't figure out what the murmuring was all about, and when it failed to cease, I walked down to the stairway which led to the basement, where I saw for the first time the Frenchman's family and a number of other people who had taken shelter in his house. There must have been at least ten of them gathered around the walls of the basement, forming a circle.

As I watched, an artillery shell came whistling overhead, and when it had passed the house, the group that had gathered in the basement began chanting the Hail Mary, which I did not know, and damn sure didn't understand. I looked at them for some time and it occurred to me that they were calling on the wrong person for help, but I didn't say anything to them. Then my eyes caught a good-looking girl about seventeen years old and I called to her, "Mademoiselle." She looked my way, and I crooked my finger, jerking it in the direction of the upstairs rooms. "Viens ici, mademoiselle."

She immediately raised herself from the potato sack on which she had been sitting and started in the direction of the stairs. When I turned to walk up before her, her father called out, "Where are you going, girl?"

Without a moment's hesitation she flipped the answer over her shoulder, "upstairs to sleep with the American soldier," and just kept walking. By golly, I thought, I've got me a hot potato who doesn't care whether Pops likes it or not. Get upstairs, mademoiselle!

I took the 16- or 17-year-old girl to a bedroom upstairs and when a fellow soldier, Simonazzi, the bazooka man from Philadelphia, saw the action, he went to the basement and did likewise. He came back with a girl and occupied the bedroom across the hall. A few moments passed, which I thought to be most blissful, then an artillery shell exploded on the roof between the two rooms. It almost tore the roof off. I jumped out of the sack, calling to Simonazzi, "We'd better get the hell out of here, Simonazzi! Let's go downstairs!"

He yelled through the door, "To hell with them! They can't do it again."

Chapter 10. Another Town to Clear

With this, I took my love and faded down the stairs to the back porch. I raked the debris that was the result of the artillery shell off the bed, then turned the covers down. My love and I slipped under them, and pulling them over our shoulders, we got after it. God, that was a sweet woman.

The next morning at about six o'clock I was awakened out of a blissful slumber by a platoon runner, who informed me that the platoon lieutenant had the men up the street, giving them instructions for the day's combat.

He told me the lieutenant was mad as a hornet at me for not being there. I got out of bed and dressed. I strapped on my gun and web belt, leaned over my love, who was fast asleep, kissed her gently, and sliding the old steel helmet over my head, I bid my love farewell. She never once stirred. She was fast asleep. As I walked up the street toward the gathered platoon, I thought of what my love had said to me the night before. I didn't understand what she had said, nor could I be expected to, for I was not an Alsace Lorrainean, nor was I as pretty as my love. "I have a brother in the French 7th Army and a brother in the Wehrmacht, mon amie. And I don't really care who wins the war."[5] God, how I hated to leave that woman.

As I approached, the lieutenant, who was standing in a circle of men in front of the barn, immediately turned his attention toward me and barked some unkind words, which I hardly noticed. Then he turned back to the men and continued to spout a bunch of nonsense about them having to carry much superfluous equipment and ammunition in an assault on the village, which was a few miles closer to the division objective of Strasbourg on the Rhine.[6]

I waited for the space of five minutes, and the longer I waited, the madder I became; finally, so mad, I began to tremble involuntarily. Then I just hauled off and stepped out into the circle beside the green nosed lieutenant who had been attached to my platoon the day before and proceeded to lay down the doctrine. I looked him full in the face and started in this fashion,

> Lieutenant, let me tell you something, goddamn it. We've been fighting this war for five months and doing pretty good before you got here. Matter of fact, you've been on the front for only three days, and during those

three days you've been transferred twice from one company to another. Now you've been pawned off on us. You came into our company yesterday and you have never so much as laid an eye on a goddamn Kraut. We've been fighting on foot most of the time and haven't been carrying too much ammunition because our half-tracks have always been within easy reach if we got in a fracas. It's been raining out there, Lieutenant, and the ground is muddy. These goddamn overshoes pick that mud up and it balls around our feet until we can hardly pick them up, let alone carry a whole bunch of unnecessary equipment. We just ain't gonna carry it, by God. And besides, the goddamn attack isn't supposed to push off until eight o'clock and it's only six now. Come on, men. Let's go get something to eat.

With this, I walked through the circle of men and headed for the company commander's post. The men fell out and disappeared in various directions, heading to their respective shelters. I made a beeline to the command post, where I told the company commander what I had done to his lieutenant. "What in the hell do you want me to do with that asshole lieutenant you sent to me yesterday, Lieutenant Gladys?"[7]

He had been in charge of the company for a short time. "See if you can't put up with him for a few days, Porter, and I'll get rid of him," he answered.

With this, I turned and left the good company commander to his business of running the company.

Gladys had treated me more than decently back in England some months before, and I liked him because he was decent to the men without fraternizing with them. I didn't like an officer who fraternized with the enlisted men. Gladys was decent without doing this. He was made company commander a few days after I took the platoon sergeant's job of corralling the third platoon, which had been without an officer for some time.

They had given the third platoon to me. I was standing in the middle of the village street where I fell in love with the young girl.

I watched, as the men of Company C assaulted a German position about a quarter of a mile away, and my platoon sergeant, whom I did not particularly care for because he had been brought in as a replacement and put in charge of the third platoon, was standing beside me. The two of us had been standing there for no more than

Chapter 10. Another Town to Clear

five minutes when a stray bullet from a German machine gun hit the sergeant in the thigh. He grabbed me by the shoulder and said, "God-damn, Porter, I'm hit!"

I slipped an arm around him at his waist and the two of us headed to the command post. I left the sergeant sitting inside the door and went to the captain, telling him our platoon sergeant had been hit. He said to me, "Leave him here and go back and take command of the platoon, Porter."

I said, "Yes sir," without too much emphasis on the sir, and went back into the house where I had fallen in love. I took a tub out of the kitchen, and filling it with water, I placed it on the stove to heat. When the water was hot, I pulled the tub down on the floor, slipped off my dirty clothing and stepped into the warm water. I bathed and shaved. I dressed and strapped on my .44 and .45, and walked into the front room, where the men of the machine gun squad slouched lazily. I stood there before a six-foot mirror, with my thumbs hooked under the leather belt supporting the two hog legs and addressed the men. "You fellers are looking at the next company commander. The old man has just made me platoon sergeant, and by God we'll have a little more respect from here on out."

The next day the dirty bastard of a company commander shipped the green lieutenant to me. *C'est le guerre, mon ami, c'est le guerre.*[8]

Then, sometime after he had made me platoon sergeant, the company commander disappeared, and Lieutenant Gladys was made company commander. They sent in another lieutenant from God only knows where and made him company adjutant under Gladys. One evening the new adjutant told Sergeant Juarez, squad leader of the first squad of riflemen, to take his track and outpost the village. He pointed out a position a hundred yards from the village and told Juarez that he should take that position, posting a guard through the night.

Juarez mounted his men, and the driver pulled the track out into the open field, where the mud very quickly gave way, causing the track to sink to its axles. The driver tried his damnedest to disentangle the machine, but to no avail. Juarez dismounted his men and

A M5 light tank of the 8th Tank Battalion being used for the evacuation of a wounded soldier. This became a common use for the light tanks when ground conditions made it difficult for wheeled vehicles or half-tracks to navigate the terrain (U.S. Army photograph).

came back to the first house on the outskirts of the village and set up guard.

Later that evening I went to pay Juarez a visit and got to drinking potato whiskey with him. It was so strong it burned blue and jerked the paint off the woodwork.

We got to feeling pretty good, and just when we were relaxed and forgot the goddamn war, the new adjutant came to the door and inquired on the whereabouts of Juarez. The man told him Juarez was in the next room, where the lieutenant walked and found Juarez and me sucking on the juice.

He stepped to within inches of Juarez and asked why he had not outposted the village, as he had been instructed. The Mexican stood up and told him what had happened, but the adjutant didn't

Chapter 10. Another Town to Clear

appreciate the excuse and proceeded to give Juarez unshirted hell for disobeying an order.

Juarez took it for a short time, then pulled out a Luger and shoved the muzzle into the adjutant's face. Looking him straight in the eye, he told him, "Listen you goddamn son-of-a-bitch. If you want this friggin' town outposted get out there in the rain and outpost it yourself. Now if you don't get the hell out of here, I'll blow your goddamn brains out!"[9]

The new lieutenant turned white as a sheet. That boy was one more scared feller, and although he desired to show his weight, he dared not take the chance. He mounted his ass and did just as the Mexican had directed, leaving the premises post haste. You can't win them all, lieutenant, better luck on the next soldier.

After Lieutenant Gladys relieved my mind of any doubt as to who was running the platoon, I went back to the machine gun section. I ate a can of C rations and went out into the street to call the men of the third platoon together, telling them what our objective for the day would be. At 8:00 o'clock sharp we fell into marching battle formation and started walking down the road toward the next village a few miles to the left.[10] The new lieutenant hadn't said anything more to me and it was just as well, for had he opened his mouth with any more orders, I would have told him to go to hell.

He took up the lead position in the middle of the road, while the platoon divided into two columns, one on either side of the road. I took up the lead position in the center of the road, which is ordinary practice, for if the leader is knocked out of action the platoon sergeant immediately moves to the front and takes command.

We walked on the road for about two hours, then took to the field in order to come up on the flank of the village we were supposed to assault. We walked about a mile cross-country before we were ordered to fan out and come to the front to form a line on the side of the lieutenant. The men very quickly ran to the front and formed the line, each man approximately five yards from his nearest companion, and I took up a position just short of them. We walked over a hill, thinking the village to be at the bottom but found that a flat field lay before us. When we reached the very top of the hill, a machine gun started spewing angry steel at us, then all hell broke loose.

The men scrambled, some of them taking to the shelter of the tall timber. One of them took a shot in the lobe of his ear and the round tore his ear off. He had just been sent to us that morning as a replacement, and now he was on his way to a hospital for a long rest.

I broke into a run and angled off to the right of the line, looking to find some kind of protection from the machine gun fire. I spotted a tower but couldn't understand why there should be a tower in the middle of that field, or what it could have been used for. All I know is that I was looking for protection and the tower seemed to be the most likely place to find it. I reached the tower and started firing into the machine gun nest, then looked around to see what had happened to the rest of the men. I was in the tower alone, but I could see that most of my men had found reasonable shelter and were returning fire. I remained in my position for five minutes, then came back to where the men were, got the lieutenant back on his feet, and we continued over the hill.

The machine gun went silent. They got the message that we were going into town, whether they liked it or not, and hauled ass. The platoon fanned out again. We started across the field in the direction of the intended assault village—and then the most peculiar sight came to our attention. A German soldier was spotted some four hundred yards to our front, and he was walking toward our line. The man was positively magnificent and most excellently alone as he marched toward us. The men were stunned and held their fire and the German soldier just kept walking. He approached our line, and without so much as looking to the right or left, he passed through it. The last time I saw that gentleman he was going over the top of the hill we had descended, taking a walk in the sun like Diogenes, who told Alexander the Great when asked if there was anything that could be done for him, "Yes. Just move from between me and the sun."

As I recall, Diogenes simply leaned back against the wall and was content to continue with his meditations. And the German soldier alone comprised the most excellent parade I have witnessed in

Chapter 10. Another Town to Clear

the 44 years of my life.[11] It took much courage for that gentleman to walk through that line. Bless his hide, wherever he may be.

Our orders were changed before we attacked the village. We changed the direction of our march to intersect the road, where we picked up our half-tracks and mounted up for a short ride through the countryside. We were riding in style instead of walking like the foot infantry was so prone to do.

The column of armor (we picked up four tanks from the 8th Tank Battalion) pulled to a stop three hundred yards from the village of Berg, when one of the tanks attempted to cross a bridge that spanned a small stream just short of the town limit.[12] The tank struck a land mine, which had been discreetly planted in the center of the road. When the mine exploded, one of the tank's tracks was torn from its mounting, completely demobilizing the machine. The tank holding the second position very quickly pulled around the disabled hunk of iron which sat on the approach of the bridge and attempted to cross the bridge. When the tank was abreast of the other, it too struck a mine that had been planted on the shoulder of the road, and now both of them were disabled and blocked the bridge completely.

The remaining tanks saw their plight and very quickly withdrew to a position approximately fifty yards to the rear. They opened fire on the village with their cannon from such short range that each time the gunners tripped the release mechanism of their respective pieces, a building on the outskirts of the village would explode into the air and crumble back to the ground a mass of debris.

My half-track had been one of the lead vehicles of the column, running directly behind the tanks of the 8th Tank Battalion. We very quickly dismounted and took up a firing position in a ditch alongside the road. By this time the Germans, who had a machine gun nest on the top of a small incline just to the left of the town, had evaluated our position, and realizing that our disabled tanks were blocking the bridge, felt it would be all right to open fire. They very discreetly had held their fire until the column had come to a stop, but now that we were halted in the middle of the road, they opened up with all the firepower they could muster. Hold on to your hats, boys. She's bucking again.

The sneaky bastards had a field piece, or I should say an anti-tank gun, going full blast on a hill opposite the position and across from their machine gun, When the machine gun started firing, they cracked down on the armor, with deadly accuracy, finding a mark each time the trigger mechanism was touched. At such range, the round struck its target at the same instant the report was heard. The dance had just begun. Do-si-do and form a line. You get yours and I'll shoot mine.

The column was flat stuck in the middle of the road just short of town, and it was damn certain the only thing left to do was dismount and attack the town on foot. Otherwise, they would sit on the top of the hill and destroy every piece of armor we had. The first platoon's first squad took the lead position in a ditch to the right of the road. The machine gun squad from the third platoon fell into the ditch behind him. The remainder of the first platoon took the ditch on the left side of the road and the balance of the column fell in behind us.

We ran across the bridge in front of the disabled tanks, and once again took to the ditches beside the road. The ditch held a foot of water, and when we reached a distance of two hundred yards from the village, the road cut at an oblique angle, shooting like an arrow, straight through the village.

The German machine gun was very busy firing into the two approaching columns of men, and a bullet struck one of the men in front of me. He grabbed his leg, fell to the bottom of the ditch, and began to roll over and over, splashing the water like a youngster playing in a shallow stream. The poor bastard was hurting but the comedy of the scene was just too much for Dutch and me. We broke up, just sitting there, having a hell of a belly laugh at the poor bastard's expense.

The second platoon was ordered to make an assault on the hill, where the Krauts were dug in with the machine gun. They crawled out of the ditch and, lining up abreast, started running across the open field in the direction of the machine gun nest, with every weapon belching a hail of fire into the hillside.

We hadn't fully realized it before we started the assault, but the Krauts had outposted the village with a line of slit trench riflemen,

Chapter 10. Another Town to Clear

Men of the 53rd Armored Infantry Battalion near Baerendorf, France, on November 25, 1944 (U.S. Army photograph).

and now that the second platoon was moving across the open field, the entrenched Krauts started firing into their line. But this didn't dampen their enthusiasm.

The men of the second platoon just crouched down, with their weapons held at their hip, and continued their funeral march. One of the Krauts got out of his trench, with his hands held in an attitude of surrender, but one of the men of the second platoon figured that the time for surrender had long since passed. He yanked back on the trigger of his M1 rifle, and the piece exploded in the guts of the surrendering Kraut. He fell back into his trench, never to make war again.

The column Dutch and I were attached to halted because of resistance at the first house, which I later found to be a Catholic church. I took John Rice, the company clown, and Dutch, and ran past the lead men of the column, trying to evaluate the position of the company. John Rice had taken to the ditch at the left of the road, while Dutch and I held to the ditch at the right. When we reached the church building, I saw what the trouble was and why the column had halted. A man, who had kicked Lieutenant Luxbacher in the ribs back at Avranches for not getting out of his trench when our position was under heavy fire, lay dead under a tree. A mortar round had hit the branches of the tree and exploded, sending a piece of shrapnel into the man's body while he crouched beneath the tree. He had been given a field promotion to the rank of second lieutenant and had led well. Now he lay very still and very dead.

I looked at the lieutenant for a second, then rounded the corner of the church building, with a grenade in my hand. The pin had been pulled as I opened the church door and tossed the grenade inside and closed the door. The grenade exploded. I opened the door and rushed inside. The smoke from the explosion filled the room but I could see the wounded Kraut, sitting with his back to the wall, clutching his belly. He was hit in the guts. Staring at him for an instant, I made the sign of the cross and went back out on the street, looking for trouble. I had John Rice, the company clown, cover the left side of the street. The two of us went from house to house, clearing them of the encroaching Krauts.

We had cleared a section of the town to a point midway up the main street before we realized we had somebody behind us who was interested in war. I had just come out of a house that had no Krauts when we saw one of our tanks coming very slowly up the street and I stopped in an open barn door to wait for the tank and to see what its crew were going to do.

The tank came abreast of my position and I watched as the commander, a second lieutenant, was dispatched in quick time and sent to the happy hunting grounds. All that could be seen of the lieutenant was his head and the topmost part of his shoulders. The driver and his assistant had the hatches buttoned over their heads, but the lieutenant was exposed. As I looked at the tank, a round of high explosive hit the leading edge of the rounded turret. The lieutenant stood for a second after the explosion, but his head had vanished. The shrapnel had torn his head from its mounting, and he fell on the

Chapter 10. Another Town to Clear

gunner's lap, a mass of blood. The gunner panicked and crawled out of the tank, then leaped to the ground and ran to the opposite side of the street.[13]

Although there was no real physical damage to the tank, it stopped when it was hit, and the crew, unbattening the hatches over their heads, crawled through the openings and leaped to the ground, then ran across the street to take shelter in the barn. Now the goddamn tank was sitting out in the middle of the street with no operator and completely exposed to the marksmanship of the Kraut gunner. Evidently, the Krauts hadn't seen the crew abandon the tank, for there were no more rounds fired upon it. They must have fired only one round and hauled ass for fear they hadn't damaged the tank too severely. Thank God for unrecognized favors, for the only round fired caused such a concussion that its force knocked me away from the open barn door and sent me hurtling through the air, as though I had been stuck full in the face with the two hind feet of a bucking bronc. I landed on my ass in back of the barn and finally came to a halt, with my ears ringing from the concussion.

Everything seemed to have happened instantaneously: the round hitting the tank turret, the officer being decapitated, and the concussion knocking me on my fanny. All as quick as a town fox snatching a chicken from the roost and escaping into the night, as positive as a bolt of lightning strikes a high voltage transformer over your head. It reminded one of the "Legend of Sleepy Hollow," in which the horseman rode through the night, his head missing and no eyes to guide him. The officer had been the head and eyes of the galloping steel steed, and when the heart had been shorn from its resting place, the crew could no longer see. They were the body and they had ceased to breathe.

The lieutenant lay very still in the street, but there was none who would venture into the street to retrieve his body.

Dutch wanted me to mount the tank and assault its killers. "To hell with it," I told him. Both of us had been trained as tank men, but a fortunate stroke of providence had placed us in a half-track together, and by the Beard of Ivan this is where I intended to stay.

After the tank incident I ran across the street to the barn, where

You're a Good Man, Sergeant

John Rice and the men from the tank were huddled in a small circle, discussing the death of the lieutenant. One of the men was relating the story to John, who had been hit in the thigh with a piece of shrapnel from the explosion.[14] I listened to them for a brief moment, then said, "Aw bullshit. The war is still going on outside and we've gotta clear this goddamn town before nightfall, or we'll be in a hell of a tough spot, trying to keep an eye on the bastards in the dark."

The crewman telling the story seemed to be all shook up because the officer had been killed, and it appeared as though he wanted somebody to sympathize with him. Hell's bells! He was still alive and had nothing to do with the dispatch of his officer, so why cry about it, unless he was prepared to get out in the street and do something to the Krauts who were responsible for the action.

I left them in the barn and worked my way up the street until I hit a house, where I thought a bunch of Krauts were hidden in the cellar. I slipped through the open front door and walked very cautiously through the house and entered the kitchen. In one corner of the empty room, I could see a door that apparently led down into the basement. I slipped across the room and gathered a bunch of pots and pans, and stacking them at the head of the steps, hauled off and gave them a hell of a kick. The pots rattled down the steps and hit the floor of the cellar with a hell of a bang. When the noise had quieted down, I called out in a loud voice, "Kommen ze rause, Kommeradden! Komen ze rause und zurrender!"

I stepped away from the open door and waited, without moving. As I waited, I made sure that the carbine was cocked and the clip full, for I was out for bear and didn't want to get caught with my bashful hanging out. Then a Kraut popped his head through the door, looked at me for an instant with a half grin spread across his face, and waited to determine what kind of mood I was in. When he saw that I intended to take him prisoner rather than kill him, he looked over his shoulder and beckoned to his comrades to alley-up. Then he stepped into the kitchen and backed against the wall, holding his hands over his head.

In less than thirty seconds, ten of them had climbed the steps and lined up against the wall beside the first man, holding their

Chapter 10. Another Town to Clear

hands over their heads. They were smiling at me as though they knew something I didn't. Maybe they were laughing at the comedy of the scene taking place, but at the moment I couldn't see anything amusing. I had allowed my sideburns to grow a full inch below my ear lobes and had shaved them to a point on the lower cheek.

I wore a steel helmet that was as shiny as a dog's nose, and the boots I wore were very definitely not regulation brogans, for they were as black as a coal bin and had hobnailed soles. Maybe what threw them was the two western smoke poles strapped around my waist, with the holsters tied down around my lower thigh. At any rate, suppose it was amusing to the Krauts to be captured by Tom Mix, which is what the French people called me when they first saw me.

I muzzled them into the front room, which had been given over to a bedroom accommodation, and asked them to throw their artillery on the bed. As they started unharnessing their guns, I kept both eyes glued to their operation, with my finger crooked around the trigger of the carbine. I was fully prepared to empty the fifteen rounds of the clip into their guts if there was any chicanery, and I seriously believe that they were aware of this intention. They threw their pistols on the bed and stepped back against the wall, where they waited to see what I would do with them. A very cooperative group of men; no trouble at all. I gathered their guns and stuffed them inside my combat jacket, which was partially unzipped and secured at the bottom with the regulation web belt I wore.

I zipped my jacket up and marched the prisoners up the street. We walked past the barn, where the tank crew was still holding their goddamn prayer meeting. When I reached the Catholic church into which I had tossed the grenade, I saw our company commander, the one who had disappeared a few days back. God only knows where he had been (probably some whorehouse in Nancy). I gave the prisoners over to his care.

He was mad as a hornet when I walked up on him. I couldn't determine what all the bullshit was about until I asked one of his men. The non-com told me that the captain was mad because the lieutenant, the one I found under the trees, was killed. The captain was looking for blood.

I walked away, only to stop and look back at the prisoners for an instant. The captain ordered them to take off their boots and tie them around their necks, preparatory to a long march back to Division, where all the prisoners were held in a compound. That chicken-shit captain was showing a streak of petty that could only be compared to the revenge of a jealous whore tearing up her sister's clothes because she has gone to bed with her pimp.

The dirty son-of-a-bitch made the Kraut prisoners walk down the road under guard in weather that wasn't fit for a dog. It was cold as a well digger's ass in Nome, Alaska. And my prisoners, being shamefully abused by that fuckin' captain was more than I cared to watch. I left feeling sorry for the barefooted prisoners and downright disgust for that chicken-shit captain.

Chapter 11

Give Me Liberty or Give Me Death

By mid-afternoon the town was cleared, and we were ordered to commandeer the houses necessary to shelter our men. I settled my men in a house that looked pretty good and went back down the road to get the half-track. When I arrived at the field where the tracks were, I discovered that our vehicle had been knocked out by a direct hit from a field cannon, probably an "88," and I went back to the chicken-shit captain, who brought up another track for me and the men of the third platoon. It arrived two hours later, and I had the driver back it into the Frenchman's barn which was connected to the house. The barn wasn't deep enough to accommodate the machine gun track, and its nose was left exposed to the sight of the Kraut artillery spotters who took immediate advantage of the opportunity.

Less than an hour after dark, the bastards opened up on the house and hit the goddamn half-track full in the nose. The explosion lit a fire in the gas tank and the whole barn exploded into an inferno. Son-of-a-bitch! There went the second track of the day! The dirty bastards were flat gunning for me, but I just sat in the Frenchman's domicile, cooking up a bunch of his chow. To hell with it!

The owner of the house came inside. He was running and out of breath. We were all scrounging around, when he told us his barn was on fire and asked us to help him put out the flames. He didn't find any takers, and proceeded to run out of the house with a firefighter's helmet, circa 1870, on his head. He crawled up on the roof, ax in hand, and began to frantically chop at a two-foot section. He worked for about thirty minutes, then came inside and told us he had saved his house, for it was made of stone. He had chopped a two-foot section of roof away from the house and the fire gnawed in vain at the stone sidewall that connected it to the barn.

The company commander had seen the fire and sent a runner to me to tell me to get the half-track out of the barn. I told the runner that there was too much ammunition exploding inside the track to get at it. He disappeared into the night, running to give the captain my message. He returned shortly, telling me, "The captain said to get that goddamn truck out of the barn. He don't care how you do it. Just get the son-of-a-bitch out of the barn."

Since the old bastard was going to get mad about it, I decided I'd better do as he commanded. I got another half-track, backed it up to within fifteen feet of the burning machine, and very cautiously threw a cable over a hook mounted on top of the bumper. We snaked the blazing funeral pyre out into the middle of the road and let the bastard light up the street. If the Krauts wanted something to shoot at, let them get after it. I went back into the house and continued with my cooking of the small pig we had taken from the owner of the house.

A lieutenant, who was a forward observer from the 66th Artillery Battalion, came to the house and asked if he and his men could move in.[1] When I gave him the okay, his men brought their gear into the house. Most of the men were in the front room, cutting up a bunch of bullshit while I was talking to the lieutenant about the position of the Krauts across the stream at the edge of town. I excused myself from the lieutenant and went into the kitchen, looking for some eggs to cook. Finding none, I went into the barn to take anything with life in it and throw it in the pot. I opened the door of the barn and saw a yearling calf. One of the lieutenant's men was standing behind the animal, with his hands grabbing at the calf's hip bones. I turned quickly and closed the door without disturbing the scene. I went into the front room and told Dutch Wanosik.

"Go out in the barn, Dutch, and see if you can find some eggs." Dutch strode out of the room, saying only, "O.K., Porter."

Within seconds, he was back in the room, laughing his ass off, and said to all the men, "That goddamn dog robbin' son-of-a-bitch is out there in the barn humpin' a calf!"

Chapter 11. Give Me Liberty or Give Me Death

The entire room broke into a roar of laughter. I hadn't meant for Dutch to spill the beans on the man, but damn his hide, he sure fixed that dog robber up, right in front of his boss, too. I knew he was going to catch hell when the story got back to his outfit.

The next morning, we were ordered to span a bridge that went over a good-sized stream, which floated past the village outskirts, and occupy a hill just a few hundred yards beyond the stream.[2] We made it to the top of the hill without any resistance, and most of the men began digging slit trenches. It had been raining for some time and I didn't feel compelled to do anything, particularly dig, so I scooped out a small gully and piled the dirt up so that it appeared that a hole had been dug. Five tanks from the 8th Tank Battalion had taken up positions around the top of the hill and we waited for the attack of one of the crack German *Panzer* divisions.

At nine o'clock that night, they hit our position with a heavy barrage. For a while, it seemed they would blow the top of the hill into dust. Everybody hit the trenches and hung tough, riding out the barrage in tense anxiety. Then the Kraut tanks began crawling up the hillside. It was raining artillery and water from the heavens, the artillery shells exploding and throwing shrapnel in all directions, and the rain kept falling, completely oblivious to the fact that there was a hell of a scramble about to take place.

When the shrapnel became too thick, I crawled under one of the tanks nearby and found that I hadn't been the only one who failed to dig a hole. A little feller by the name of Jiminez, a Latin from California, had thought it was a pretty good idea, and now the two of us lay under the tank, waiting for the attack.[3] I told him we would look for a hole to crawl in when the artillery stopped for a second. He agreed. Within five minutes, they lifted the barrage, and we started running across the top of the hill, heading for a long trench that the Krauts had dug before they left the area. The trench snaked around the military slope of the hill that was nearest the village. Therefore, we were taking a lesson in strategic retreat.

We had run a hundred yards or so, when the bastards hit the top of the hill again with a mean ass barrage. A shell hit the ground fifty feet from me and let out a hell of a roar, and a piece of shrapnel whizzed through the air and struck me full on the right cheek of my rump. My leg went numb.

Oddly enough, all I could think of was how guilty I felt at the thought of leaving the men of the third platoon. Jiminez heard the slap of the shrapnel against the rubber raincoat, and I must have cursed aloud about being hit, for he continued over the top of the hill and made it to a trench, where my men were told I had been hit.

I ran my hand under my belt and felt for blood, which I expected, but was greatly relieved to discover that the shrapnel had struck flat, rather than on edge. The blow had only temporarily paralyzed my right leg, and I limped across the top of the hill in time to hear the men passing the news that I had been hit. "Porter got hit," I could hear them say, as they passed the statement along.

I slid into the trench and stayed there for a few minutes, thinking of the mess we were in. While I lay there, the company commander and his gang came into my mind. I didn't like the idea of them being back in those warm houses. I did not like it worth a damn. If we had to be out in the cold, it was good enough for the whole shebang. I climbed out of the trench and started down the hill. To hell with that hill! If the company commander wanted it, he could take it himself. If the Krauts wanted the son-of-a-bitch, let them have it. As for me, I would take the village.

I ran across the bridge to a barn I thought to be unoccupied, but as I stepped through the door, I could hear a man groaning and I knew he had been wounded. By this time the Kraut tanks had started up the hill again, their supporting artillery laying a barrage down on the village. The armor was moving up under cover of the barrage, and I knew the men on top of the hill were going to take a hell of a licking if they didn't get out of there, but if they didn't have the sense or the courage to get a move on when the fire got too heavy, let them suffer the consequences.

As for me, give me liberty or give me death, and I had sense enough to take the liberty of getting off that damned hill before the fire got to blazing.

I stood in the darkness of the barn for a brief moment, then walked in the direction of the groan. Two men were gathered around

Chapter 11. Give Me Liberty or Give Me Death

another, who lay on the floor of the barn, and lifted a ten-inch beam off his chest.

Moments before, an artillery shell had exploded on the barn roof and loosed the beam, which had acted as a floor joist for the loft, and it had fallen on the man's chest, caving in his rib cage. I looked at the wounded man for an instant, then realized I could do no more than the other two men were already doing and went out into the darkness.

The rain was coming down steadily. I buttoned the slicker (it was that of a German officer) around my neck and started moving down the street, hugging close to the buildings and trying to be as inconspicuous as possible. I reached the middle of the village before anything happened, then the Krauts cranked up their goddamn artillery again and laid most of it right in the middle of the village.

"Son-of-a-bitch! Ain't there anywhere a man can get away from that gang?"

I ran into another barn, and backing against the wall, remained there for thirty minutes while the shrapnel and rain filled the angry air around the village. Touché you bastards, fight brave and long. As for me, I'll take the barn. It feels pretty good.

I could hear great noises from atop the hill, where I'd been hit, and I knew that it wouldn't be long before my men got the message and got the hell out of there. I sat in the barn for a full thirty minutes, and when the artillery lifted, I went back out on the wet street and continued my strategic retreat in the direction of the command post and the company commander.

When I reached the house where he and his men were holed up, I walked in like I owned the joint. They seemed to be preoccupied with some business, which didn't seem too important to me, so I walked across the room to a corner, where a stove was glowing red from the fire inside it and slid down on my butt. I just sat there, saying nothing, and minding my own business. I hoped that the good officers present had sense enough to do the same, for I wasn't prepared to listen to a bunch of bullshit.

An hour after my arrival at the command post, a sergeant brought in a prisoner and a lieutenant from G-2, who started questioning him about the mines that had been planted down by the bridge where two of our tanks had been knocked out of action.[4]

The sergeant who had captured the Kraut seemed to be trying to impress the good captain with his willingness to obey orders and his desire to do in the prisoner. More importantly, the dumb bastard was trying to win recognition from a bunch of assholes who didn't even recognize the nose on their goofy faces. But he didn't know how goddamn goofy the sonsabitches were and continued to lend his assistance to the interrogation by saying to the captain, "Let me take him out and shoot him. If he won't answer the questions let me take him out and shoot him."

He was willing to kill a man to impress the officers on whom I would not piss.

The prisoner told the lieutenant from G-2 that he had been one of the groups who planted the mines. When the captain heard this, he immediately told the lieutenant to inform the Kraut that he was going to show our engineers the whereabouts of the mines, and that he would also have the privilege of removing them. The lieutenant, acting as translator, informed the Kraut of what the company commander had said, and the Kraut became very nervous and told the lieutenant that the fuses could not be lifted out of the mines without exploding them, as they were extremely sensitive. "I don't give a damn how sensitive they are," the captain shouted. "That son-of-a-bitch put them there and two of our tanks were knocked out. Tell this bastard he'll either take the fuses out, or I'll let this man shoot him on the spot," he continued, pointing his finger at the sergeant, whose chest raised a full six inches at the attention he was finally getting.

I said nothing, but I didn't like the chicken-shit sergeant worth a damn because I knew him to be a chicken-shit bastard, just like the captain who made the ten prisoners take off their boots and walk to Division in the mud and cold of winter.

But the interrogating lieutenant from G-2 had more sense than anyone else in the room. He quickly rose to the defense of the prisoner, saying, "This cannot be permitted. I am sending the prisoner back to Division for further interrogation. He has valuable

Chapter 11. Give Me Liberty or Give Me Death

information concerning the concentration of German troops across the river, and since we are under attack by a *Panzer* division, it is extremely important that we question him in the hopes he might disclose the positions of other *Panzer* concentrations."

The night wore on and the interrogation continued, with the captain and the sergeant showing a bravado that was nothing more than bullshit, and the lieutenant could see right through it.

Daylight finally started creeping over the village and troops were seen moving around with much caution, for they weren't really sure who was occupying the village. There'd been a hell of a scramble on the top of the hill during the early part of the night, and most of the men had abandoned the hilltop for the shelter of the village houses.

I moved my operation from behind the stove, and slipping out onto the awakening street, started looking for the rest of the third platoon. By mid-day, I had gathered the men of the third platoon into the house, where we sat for another day, licking our wounds, and counting the missing men that failed to make it back over the bridge.

One of the men, a Frenchman from lower Louisiana, Bonvillain by name, ran off the hilltop when the shooting got too hot for him to handle. Instead of going across the bridge dry-shod, he jumped into the stream and swam across it to the opposite side, where he remained in the water until morning. He was not sure whether or not the Krauts had taken over the village and was afraid to venture into town. The poor bastard caught himself a bad case of pneumonia and was sent to the rear, where he remained for the duration of the war. After he got to the hospital the psychiatrist reclassified him, giving him some kind of neurosis, and we never heard from him again.[5]

Another youngster from the Cajun Country in Louisiana started moving around the top of the hill, when the going got a little tough. He was caught in an artillery barrage while looking for the men he thought to be still there. He jumped into a foxhole with his platoon sergeant and sat there for some time before he realized the sergeant was dead.

At the same time, a German infantryman walked up to the hole and looked very intently down on the two men, both of whom he thought to be dead. The Cajun, however, was very much alive, and as he was in a squatting position, with the muzzle of his rifle in an upright attitude, his natural impulse was to pull the trigger and belch out a flame of hot lead into the German's face. But he had left the safety in a locked position, and nothing of an angry disposition happened. So, he sat very quietly in the hole as the Kraut walked away, much to the relief of the coon-ass from Louisiana.

When the Kraut had disappeared, the kid from the Cajun Country snaked out of the hole on his belly, crawled for a hundred feet, and jumped to his feet and disappeared down the hillside in a hell of a rush. If anybody got in his way, he'd yell, "If that's the fastest you can move, step aside. I'm in a real rush!"

Late that evening I was standing in front of the house, when a sergeant drove up in a jeep and asked me, "Do you know where I can find Dutch Wanosik?"

I answered that Dutch was one of my men and that he was down the street, goofing off. I told him I'd be glad to fetch Dutch for him if he would wait in the house. As I went in search of Dutch, the sergeant dismounted and went inside. I found Dutch in a barn down the street and told him his brother was at the house waiting to see him. He tore off down the street in a hard run. I was curious to see what their reactions would be, so I followed the Pole, and when he hit the steps and saw his brother standing in the doorway, he tripped all the way to the top, where his brother waited. They threw their arms around each other and stood there, slapping each other on the back for a full three minutes before they looked at each other. Dutch was crying tears as big as a horse turd and couldn't stop saying, "Son-of-a-bitch. Well, I'll be goddamn. Son-of-a-bitch. Well, I'll be goddamn."

Chapter 12

A Godforsaken Village

The next morning, Company B was given another village to capture. We mounted the half-tracks and, lining up in convoy formation, we pulled out of the village. Possession of the house was returned to its owner, and although he may have thought that we took advantage of his hospitality, we left him in far better shape than he had been in, for the Krauts had occupied the village for four years. He could rest assured that there would be no Heiney soldier in his domicile again. He might say with the signifying monkey, "I'm free. At last, I'm free."

The formation of armor moved across the bridge, two tank destroyers in the lead position. A quarter mile beyond the bridge, the forward observer, who was riding point in a jeep, spotted a German tank and raced back to inform the destroyer command of his find.

One of the destroyers moved very cautiously up the road to a vantage point and cracked down on the German tank with a round of armor piercing ammunition. The first round hit the tank square in the nose, and its crew jumped out of their machine and raced over the nearest hill with their coat tails flying in the breeze.

The column of armor moved past the tank and raced toward the next village, our objective, only a few miles away. The column stopped a mile short of the village and the infantry dismounted along either side of the road. We were going to assault the town, with the tanks hanging back to serve as artillery.

The third platoon, along with what was left of the second, fell off approximately two hundred yards to the left of the road, while the remainder of the company took the other side of the main road, leading into the village. When we reached the edge of the wooded area where the terrain opened into a field, we were making a pincer movement against the village.[1] The tanks opened up with their cannon and bombarded the town for five minutes. Then, when the artillery stopped, we crossed the field in a flying line formation. This means we were lined up abreast of one another, not walking, but galloping across the field, which we did without incident. The Krauts had felt the sting of the artillery, and figuring us for an attack, hauled ass.

We moved into the town, where we regrouped and were ordered into combat columns, each man five yards from his nearest companion. We walked out of the village to assault the Krauts, who had dug in a half mile beyond it. We reached the top of a hill that sloped very gently from the edge of town and went into a line formation, spreading out across the entire field, which had been planted with some kind of grain.

Not being sure of the Krauts' position, we moved ever so cautiously across the top of the hill until we were midway across the open field. Then it was "Katie bar the door," for the dirty military bastards had waited until we were in the middle of the field, where there was no avenue of escape, then let us know of their whereabouts in no uncertain terms. They hit us with three machine guns they had dug in on the other side of the valley.

We were hopelessly pinned down, and to cap it off, they started lobbing mortar down on us just for the hell of it. The machine gun bullets whizzed overhead, some of them kicking up mud around us, and when the mortar shells started exploding, I thought we had had our day in the sun.

I thank God I'm here to tell the world that I was scared stiff. We lay there in the middle of the field for the better part of five minutes, with all hell breaking loose, then I had a sudden urge to move out of my position. I don't know who or what prompted me to move, but I rolled over a few times and stopped, with my belly hugging a furrow that was no more than four inches deep. I felt as safe as if I were in a trench ten feet deep.

I had no sooner come to a stop, when a mortar tube from across the valley spit out a round. The projectile shot into the air and came to a stop a hundred yards over my head. The fins flipped skyward,

Chapter 12. A Godforsaken Village

and the round plummeted earthward, giving off a whooshing sound, which caused cold chill bumps to rise on the surface of my body. I stiffened out and clawed at the earth, for I knew the round was going to crash in the center of my back. The shell hit the exact spot from which I had just moved, and exploded with a hell of a roar, sending shrapnel in all directions. I could not have been more than ten feet from where the round exploded, and as it had made its final descent, my body grew so tense that, had I been hit, I would have shattered like a glass on a concrete floor. Thank the Lord for sending me the message to roll off that knoll.

A mortar shell hits the ground and explodes in a saucer pattern, sending the main body of shrapnel in an arching movement away from the center. Had it not been for the saucer-like pattern peculiar to mortar explosions, the grave registration boys would have picked me up with a vacuum cleaner and I'd be in Valhalla, watching the damn fools of the world fight with each other right now.

The company commander realized what position we were in and called for the tanks to come forward. They pulled up almost to the crest of the hill and opened up with machine gun fire. They were on the military slope of the hill, which caused their fire to move past our heads at an altitude of less than three feet. Now we were pinned flatter than a flitter from the fire coming in on us from our tanks and the Krauts, making it impossible for us to move in any direction. Hold it in. 'er, Newt, and it'll all be over in a minute.

The tank commander finally got his brain to working and ordered his gunners to load their cannon with phosphorous smoke rounds, and when they exploded in the valley below, a curtain of white smoke rose in the air. We remained in our positions for a minute. When the smoke had filled the valley, we jumped to our feet and ran like a herd of stampeded white-faced cattle back over the hill. We passed the tanks without so much as a thank you and headed for the brush country a good hundred yards to their rear.

Goddamn that operation and to hell with the slow thinking bastards that took half an hour to make up their minds to lay down a simple smoke screen. If West Point trains their officers to think so quickly when caught in an untenable situation as simple as the one we were in, then it would probably be much better to staff the school with a bunch of farm boys. They at least would have sense enough to get inside when it started raining.

The company gathered on the road a hundred yards to the rear of the tanks and started moving back down the hill to the village that snuggled close to the hillside, where we had almost met the maker of our souls. As we marched down the hillside, we met a jeep which was making its way in the direction of the hilltop, where we had left the tanks. As the jeep passed my position, I recognized a first lieutenant that had been my platoon commander back in Fort Knox, Kentucky, almost a year and a half gone by. "Hey there, Lieutenant," I called to him, "where in the hell do you think you're going?"

He looked at me for a moment and said, "Hello there, Porter. What the hell you fellows run into up there on that hill?"

The driver of the jeep pulled to a halt, and I walked to the side of the vehicle and engaged the lieutenant in conversation. He told me he was commander of the tank destroyers that were on the hilltop engaging the Kraut tanks in an artillery duel. The Krauts had moved up a tank or two just prior to our evacuation of the position on the hill, and now they sat across the valley, sporadically belching deadly fire, trying to knock the lieutenant's tank destroyers in the creek.

I told the lieutenant where the fire was coming from. We talked for a minute or two, and then he moved toward the top of the hill to take immediate command of the situation. It made me feel good to see that man and to know that he was enjoying a little freedom away from the spit and polish routine of Fort Knox. Hell of a price to pay for freedom, but in the realization of freedom there must always be a price. It was worth the effort applied, and even though we sent many a Kraut to Valhalla in our efforts to enjoy freedom, lasting only as long as we're on the firing line, the end justified the means, or so I would prefer to believe.

We reached the village at the foot of the hill and immediately set about to commandeer housing for our troops.[2] I took up residence with the third platoon in the first house on the street. We set out to forage wood for the fire and meat for the table. The Krauts had left a few chickens in the yard, but Dutch, who had found a derby hat and

Chapter 12. A Godforsaken Village

walking cane, put a quick end to their troubles, along with the troubles of a duck that didn't seem to know there had been one hell of a price paid on the hill for his dear body.

Dutch wore the derby very proudly and wielded the cane with much dexterity, chasing after the fowl. He hooked the rounded handle of the cane around their necks, pulling them to him and striking off their heads with the deft stroke of an accomplished swordsman.

I left the house and walked to the Catholic church a block away and entered, looking for candles that might bring a little light to the men who had been on the edge of Hades.[3] I found eight or ten candles and pocketed them. I was making my way to the door when a voice sounded behind me, "American swine! Why do you rob the church of her candles?"

"For light, your stupid son-of-a-bitch," I called to the voice, turning in its direction as the reproach left my lips. When I was fully turned in the direction of the voice, I was looking a black-robed priest in the face, but he didn't shake me worth a goddamn. I looked at him for an instant, then turned and went out onto the street, without saying another word to him. I felt satisfied at the reproach I had directed to the good man who labored with his mouth, but he didn't have too much to offer in the way of necessity.

I thought of what I might have said to him: "Hellfire, man! This is a time for action. Better get on your knees and hightail it out of this God forsaken village, or the Krauts will give you more than ample reason to support such action, when they find out we Americans are encamped here."

All this and more ran through my mind, as I walked to the house, where Dutch and the men of the third platoon had started cooking the duck and chickens that Dutch had taken as a bounteous gift from on high.

I couldn't figure the priest. Why was he still in the village, when all his flock had mounted their asses and left? Why wasn't he with his flock? They were scattering to the four winds, and he sat there in the church building, piously guarding a few half-burned candles and numerous rows of empty pews that held nothing more than the memories of faces, looking up at him from out of the past. Well, if that is where he wanted to be, to hell with him. Every man to his own liking. Like the forward observer's dog robber back in the firefighting Frenchmen's barn, making love to a yearling calf. If he wanted to remain there and run the risk of being sent to the kingdom to come, prematurely, then so be it. For the freedom which I enjoyed, I would not deny another.

The next morning, we mounted up on a road at the village outskirts and went back up the hillside. We looked the situation over for a minute, then pushed headlong down into the valley and into the woods, where the Krauts had been dug in the previous day.[4] We didn't run into too much fire until we entered the wooded area on the side of the opposing hill. But where?

We were part way through the forest when the sonsabitches ran up a tank and started firing directly into the trees. As the high explosives hit the tops of the trees, all hell with its accompanying sirens of death was set loose in our midst. The shrapnel was singing through the trees with angry buzzing that reminded us that it wasn't bees a-buzzin', cousin.

We ran through the remaining forest as quickly as possible, what with the shrapnel and the treetops falling around us making our progress slow and uncertain. We reached the edge of the trees, where we found that our tank destroyers had literally knocked the hell out of a *Tiger* tank that had hugged close to the tree line the day before. Now it lay motionless, with the long barrel of its cannon slumped down to within a few feet of the ground. The round had hit alongside where the gasoline tanks were hidden under an inch or so of armor and set the monster afire.

The round must have pierced the inside of the tank because the fire had literally gutted the inside, not allowing time for the crew to abandon it. The tank commander was stretched out on the back of the machine like barbecued pork. He must have been hit by the incoming shrapnel. However, he had had the presence of mind to realize the tank was finished and had crawled out of the top hatch, where he was caught in a blazing inferno. Now he lay there under the darkened sky on the tank that had caused us so much misery, as though he had been offered in sacrifice to the oncoming

Chapter 12. A Godforsaken Village

barbarians, who now laid claim to the land he had stolen in the first place.

I crawled up the side of the burned monster and looked down the top hatch, and what met my eyes was not for babes to look upon. The crew were still in their respective positions of command, as though awaiting orders to crank up their machine of destruction and be on their way. They sat there in silence, not knowing, not feeling, not seeing, not hearing, for they were all very dead. Their clothing had burned away very quickly, leaving only their flesh to supply the fuel for the angry fire that blazed inside the tank. They sat at their controls inside the tank, cooked to the bone, while their commander had met the same fate on the back of the charred piece of armor, staring through holes where once had been eyes, at the dark sky above. Kaput.

It was there at the edge of the forest that I witnessed the carrying away of a mess sergeant who had been in charge of the cooks that prepared our meals back in Devizes, England, where we made our happy homes for better than seven months. The dehydrated food they slapped together like so much slop for hogs wasn't exactly what you might call appetizing. They had studied very well the art of adverse food preparation. It was lousy. Well, one evening back then, I sneaked through the kitchen to the storeroom and slipped a length of salami in my trouser leg. I was halfway through the window, three feet off the floor, when this hairy-assed mess sergeant caught me by the leg and tried to pull me back through the window. I gave him a hell of a kick and fell through the window, stealing off into the night. I ran still holding the salami I had risked digging another six-by-six for, for had the C.O. been apprised of this action I would surely have dug him another hole in the ground. That man was unable to break me like a bronc, but he sure did try.

The mess sergeant had evidently grown tired of hearing the combatants talk of the war up front and had thrown in with the men of Company C. Now as I walked out of the forest, two stretcher bearers ran past me with the mess sergeant aboard. They didn't stop, for they were in a hell of a hurry to get him to a hospital. He had been hit by shrapnel and was bleeding like a stuck hog. Now he understood why I stole that stick of salami, but back in England he could have had no way of knowing what we were preparing for. It had been a dog-eat-dog position from the first day I went into the army.

Those who were in command ate well and slept well, while the dog faces ate what they had left over, so to speak. They skimmed the cream off the top of the barrel and left the skimmed milk for the dog faces. Democracy? My big ass!

But those in command in the communist countries do likewise. They skimmer down and give what is left to the dog faces. But now that we were in combat, the bastards ate what we ate and slept under similar conditions. Now they were paying for their prior gravy train operation, and still, many of them didn't know their ass from a hole in the ground. They didn't know because as soon as we'd make it to the rear, they'd start the same old bullshit over again.

We moved out across the field and took up a defensive position, digging our trenches for the night. Boy, it was cold as a wet rock. It had been raining and the terrain was drenched, so were the men drenched and tired from the day's action. It was dark and everybody was edgy and pissed off. We ate "K" rations and griped.[5] A few of the men came to me and I wrote them a slip of white paper, and they went to the rear for battle fatigue, and I didn't give a goddamn. Let the hair go with the hide, Sam, for I was trying to ship as many to the rear as would come to me and ask. I figured if I sent enough of them back, they would relieve our company and we'd get off that friggin' line for a few days.

But all this effort was wasted, for the next day we mounted the back of a platoon of tanks from the 8th Tank Battalion and we made an assault on the village of Domfessel, Alsace-Lorraine.[6] We mounted the back of the tanks, seven men to a tank, and rolled through the countryside until we came to the outskirts of the village. Then we took to the fields, making an assault from the top of the hill that overlooked it.

The tank I was riding rolled over the top of the hill and there before us, seventy-five yards away, was a Kraut machine gun nest with two jaspers caught inside. They couldn't run, for our tanks had caught them red handed. It was either shoot, Luke, or give up your gun.

Chapter 12. A Godforsaken Village

The two of them elected to hightail it down the hill. They crawled out of their entrenchment, made of rocks, and tore ass down the hill, heading for the village. The cannon of the tank bucked and one of the machine gunners disintegrated. The round of high explosives hit the ground just under his feet and the Kraut man just blew to pieces.

The other gunner made it to a house and disappeared inside. We, the armored infantry, dismounted on the outskirts of the village and scrambled our way into an orchard, where we took refuge behind the trees. They weren't so very big but they seemed like veritable walls of steel. The Krauts inside the village had heard the commotions and started small arms fire in our direction. I was one more scared son-of-a-bitch, for we were caught out in the open orchard and the music was playing a real jig time tune.

Lying there behind an apple tree for the space of three minutes, I surveyed the situation, scared to death, but the music just kept playing. One of our tanks pulled past our position and rumbled down an alley, coming to a stop just short of the main street that divided the village in the middle. I looked from my position behind the small apple tree and mustered up the necessary courage to leap to my feet and run down the hill to the spot where the tank had rumbled to a stop.

Just as I reached the tank, a German soldier ran around the corner of a house into the alley and spotted a group of us old G.I.s standing beside the tank. He threw up his hands in an attitude of surrender and one of the men grabbed him by the arm and pushed him into the alley. Then I saw a man who was really scared. The tank was too wide to maneuver through the alley and the driver placed the right track on a short wall, canting the machine at a 45-degree angle, which made an opening under the right side of the tank big enough for a man to run under if he were in a crouched attitude. The German soldier had run under the tank, which was pulling further out onto the main street in order to traverse his fire laterally, when I reached out and grabbed him by the shoulder and literally threw him into the open door of the house.

The tank pulled far enough out in the street to traverse his fire and blasted a few rounds into the houses on the opposite side of the street. I took the men from the machine gun squad and moved quickly across the street, where we ducked into the first house.

I had told a staff sergeant, who led the first squad, to take his men and clean out the houses on the nearest side of the street. I further instructed him to follow me and my men as closely as possible, for if he did not, our left flank would be exposed.

I left the house and ran a few paces up the street and opened the door of an adjacent house. I threw a hand grenade, which was spewing like a rattlesnake, inside and closed the door. The grenade went off with a hell of a roar and I grabbed the doorknob and rushed inside.

When I entered the room, the carbine I carried at my hip was barking. I stopped when I had, like a hound close on the heels of a tiring fox, gained the middle of the room. I looked around for a second before I spotted the Kraut soldier, standing behind a piece of furniture that stood slightly away from the corner of the wall.

He looked at me for an instant, then walked to the center of the room, where he stood before me. I gave him a quick shake down and left him standing in the middle of the room. He was completely dumbfounded, as I turned and walked back on the street again. His teeth had been yanked and all the fight had gone out of him, so I just left him to do whatever came to his tired, little mind.

I started up the street again, and now John Rice and the rest of the men were behind me. I looked across the street but didn't see the men of the first squad, so I called out to John to take over. I returned to the house where we had left the men of the first squad and found that they hadn't even left the house. I told the sergeant I would shoot his ass if he didn't get his men out on the street and clear the houses on his side. With this, I left and continued to where I had left John in charge of the men of the machine gun squad.

We cleared a few more houses before I took notice that the men of the first squad weren't across the street. I asked John to come with me and we returned to the house occupied by the first squad. They were still there, scared to death. "You sorry son-of-a-bitch," I yelled at the sergeant. "Damn you! From now on consider yourself a private,"

Chapter 12. A Godforsaken Village

I continued, pointing my finger at John Rice. "This man is going to take over your squad."

I left John with the men of the first squad, and he immediately ordered them out into the street. I crossed to the other side of the street and looked around. Old John was hot on my heels with his men close on his. We stopped for a few minutes in a house just short of the street corner and I went upstairs to see if any of the Krauts had taken to hiding with the upstairs maid. When I returned downstairs, John and his men weren't there. I gained the street again, and walked to the corner house, and just as I reached the barn, John Rice ran in, in a stooped position, calling to me, "My God, Porter! I'm hit!"

With this, he fell to the ground at my feet. "Where are the dirty sonsabitches that shot you, John?" I asked him as I stooped to look at his wound.

My hands were very busy tearing his shirt away from his chest, and as I looked at the clean, round hole the bullet had made in his right upper chest, he said to me, "Across the street, Porter. In the corner house."

His voice trembled as he spoke the words to me. I couldn't hide the pent-up anger that swelled within me, nor the love that I held for old long-nosed John.

I started trembling involuntarily, and big tears began rolling down my face right there in front of John, and I didn't give a damn. I loved that bastard, and now he lay there before me, shot by a son-of-a-bitch who was holed up in a house across the street.

I ran out of the barn in much haste, running across the street in search of the dirty bastard who shot old long-nosed John. I was one more mad Okie son-of-a-bitch, as I ran to the side door that opened into the kitchen of the house from which John had been shot.

I stopped in the doorway for a fraction of a second, and damned if there wasn't a Kraut standing smack in the middle of the room with his rifle held at his side, pointing straight at my knees. He jerked the trigger back and the rifle kicked up, belching a cloud of black smoke and a round that was meant for me. The bullet struck the ground at my side and sung off into the great beyond, and I turned and threw myself into the barn with the rest of the livestock.

I hadn't paid too much attention as to where I might land, but when I regained my faculties, I found myself stretched out under a milk cow, her tits hanging over my face. Unlike some women, she didn't seem to care whether I saw them or not.

I crawled under her belly, scrambled out of the barn on all fours, then straightened up to my feet and ran to a window that gave a full view of the kitchen. I raised the carbine up to the window and pointed the muzzle toward the open kitchen door. I started yanking the trigger in rapid fire. When the firing pin gave me the dull thud that told me the clip was empty, I pulled the pin from a grenade and sailed the deadly little toy into the kitchen for the amusement of the Heiney soldier, with love and kisses from John Rice.

As soon as the hand grenade was free of my hand and sailing, I reached for another clip and jammed it into the carbine, pulling the bolt back to fill the chamber with another round, as I rounded the corner of the barn. When I reached the side of the door, the grenade exploded. Then I jumped to the center of the room, firing the carbine at my side as I entered. But there wasn't a soul in the room. The kitchen window was open, and the breeze caused the curtains to move ever so gently.

I looked out the window but saw no one. I pulled a trap door in the center of the kitchen and looked down into a kind of cellar affair, but all I could see in the immediate light was apples and potatoes. I pulled the pin from another grenade and let it fall into the cellar. While the grenade spewed down in the cellar, I walked through the open door into the barn. The grenade let out a hell of a blast and I walked back into the room and called into the cellar, "Komen ze rouse, und surrender, Komrad."

But nobody came out. I waited for a few minutes, then walked back to the barn across the street, where John Rice was still bleeding like a butchered hog. I tried to comfort him as much as possible, then walked back to the open door of the barn to look across the street where I had had the fracas with the Heiney soldier.

As I looked around the corner, I noticed a white flag waving from the cellar window that had been knocked out. I walked back across the street and called to them to come out. Fifteen of them walked out

Chapter 12. A Godforsaken Village

of the house and gave up like good little boys. I walked them across the street and gave them to Capo, who had been guarding about fifty prisoners we had taken earlier. Capo was the little feller who had shot the medic back at Avranches. He was still hanging in there and I think he was enjoying every minute of it.

A couple of days prior to the action of taking the village, the company commander had put another lieutenant in charge of the third platoon. His name was Farmer and he was a very good man, as he respected the experienced men of the company who had been in action since Normandy.[7]

Now the lieutenant gathered a few of us in the barn, where John Rice lay wounded, and explained the ultimate objective of the third platoon. We were to go through the village and take a railroad bridge which was to the east of the village, some three hundred yards or so. When the critique was finished, Lieutenant Farmer took the lead and ran across an open field, crossing a barbed wire fence in the process, while we followed on his heels.

The Krauts had a machine gun set up in a church steeple two hundred yards to our right flank, and as we ran across the open field, the gunner did his damnedest to improve his marksmanship, for he raked the field without ceasing. But we managed to gain the bridge without a single casualty.

When we arrived at the bridge, which was very short and no more than twenty feet wide, we gathered under it, where we sat in water a foot deep for a few minutes, appraising the futility of risking so much manpower in order to insure such a trivial piece of real estate.

I sat there for no more than five minutes, if that long, looking at the men who had crossed the field with me to capture the bridge, and hearing the sporadic fire back in the western section of the village, I began to think of old John Rice. Again, I tried not to, but couldn't help but feel that I had deserted him. After all, if I did not help him, who would? I said to my comrades, "To hell with this bullshit! I ain't sitting here under this goddamn bridge, getting my ass wet with all that fracas going on in the village!"[8]

With that, I raised myself out of the shallow creek and started running back across the open field, while the Kraut machine gunner did his best to get my range. The bullets whizzed over my head and smacked into the sodden earth around me, but this dumb Okie had enough jack rabbit in him to avoid getting caught in the gunner's sights. Besides, I had to get back to John. He needed me.

Dutch Wanosik, the Polish dumb guy I ran with most of the time, followed close behind me, and when the two of us reached the village outskirts, we stopped to catch a breath in front of a garage, which had been stuccoed. Before you could say Jack Sprat, the goddamn Kraut gunner spotted us and turned a hail of angry little pellets loose in our direction. The bullets sprayed against the wall behind us, and I could feel the small pieces of disintegrating metal spraying against my trouser leg. This broke up the chitchat we had engaged in while standing there, and we tore ass across the street to the barn, where John Rice hung tough.

When I saw that his condition had worsened, I began to get even more concerned about John than I had already been. I left the barn in search of a medic that had an ambulance at his disposal. I wanted very much to get John out of that barn and send him to the nearest hospital. If he wasn't operated on soon, he would surely cash in his chips in the barn.

I ran down the street in the direction of Company C. They were given the task of clearing the westernmost half of the village, and this was the direction in which I had to travel in search of the ambulance. The road to the rear and the field hospital came into the village from the west. I had to either go through the village or skirt around it in order to find the ambulance I wanted so very much for John Rice.

I reached the center of the village, where my company had entered without mishap, but this time I ran into a group of men in a barn a few houses to the west of the alley where all the bullshit had started. All of them, without exception, were bleeding from the guts or the head. They were in the barn completely helpless, and there were none of their able-bodied men present to guard or look after them.

I knew one of the wounded men, and after inquiring as to his condition, I asked him where all the damage had come from. He told

Chapter 12. A Godforsaken Village

me that there was a sniper in the house just in front of the barn. But I had John Rice on my mind at the moment and didn't attempt to put a silencer on the bastard in the house. Unfortunately, I had to leave the wounded men there.

I left the barn by the back door and started across an open field to the north of the village, but only progressed a short distance when I saw a major by the name of Crosby, our battalion adjutant.[9] He was standing in the middle of the field, gazing very intently at the ground, while the fracas was bursting all around him. I walked up to where he stood and looked at his feet to see what held his attention. He was looking down at a pool of blood, just standing there with a .45 automatic held in his right hand, which hung limply at his right side.

"Major," I said to him. "You've got to get out of this open field, or you'll get shot."

The suddenness of the remark and the hidden plea caused him to snap out of the quandary, and he turned to look at me. "Where is your commander, sergeant? Where is his command post?" he asked in two very calm queries. I answered, "Come with me, Major. I'll show you where his half-track is."

With that I started back across the field in the direction of the barn, where the men of Company C lay wounded. When we reached the barn, I explained to the major that Company C had been given the objective of clearing out

(Then) 1st Lieutenant Henry Crosby, pictured in the 1942 Pine Camp book. Crosby would eventually be promoted to the rank of major and serve as the S-3 for the 53rd Armored Infantry Battalion (U.S. Army photograph).

the western section of the village but had been hampered by the machine gunner in the church steeple, who had done more than his share of damage to the men of that company.[10] Company C had been held up, I told the major, because all of their noncoms had been either killed or wounded, and the men were slouching around, just waiting to be told what to do.

After we had talked with some of the wounded sergeants, I told the major that I would have a look in the house in front of the barn and give him a report on my findings. I raced across the short distance that separated the barn from the house where the men had been wounded. The carbine jerked in my hands as it exploded a rapid fire into the back door of the house I intended to enter. Screaming like a Comanche on fire water, I leaped through the open door to find myself staring straight down a hallway that split the house in the center. All the doors leading into the rooms on either side of the hall were closed, but the front door was swung upon, making it possible to look from one end of the house to the other from either direction.

Two very still forms lay in the otherwise vacant hallway. The mortal remains of two men from Company C who had been shot as they came into the open front door that framed them for death. I looked at their dead bodies for an instant, thinking of John Rice, then went through the house room by room, but found absolutely nothing of a hostile nature. I went to the back of the hallway and opened a door that led down into the cellar and called, "Komen ze rouse, kommeraden!"

I stood waiting but a few moments before a group of French citizens walked to the hall where I stood. I herded them out the back door and ran them across the yard to the barn, where the major was still waiting. After I told him of the men inside and where the fire that killed them and wounded the others was coming from, the major asked me to take him to my command post.

We left the barn and continued to the captain's half-track, where I left the major and then went to look in again on John Rice. He was still hanging tough. I left right away to go back through the village in search of an ambulance, for it was quite obvious that old John could not hang tough much longer.

Chapter 12. A Godforsaken Village

I stopped outside the barn to talk with Capo for a few seconds, and while we talked, he kept glancing in the direction of the front of the barn, where by now 65 German prisoners were lined up, with their backs to the wall. I turned, facing the prisoners, and saw why Capo was glancing in their direction, not moving his head but shooting glances in their direction with a lateral movement of the eyes only.

One of the prisoners had been inching his way toward the open barn door, swinging his toes to the right, then bringing his heels in the same direction until they were in line with his toes, but ever so smoothly and deceitfully. As not to be noticed by an unskilled hunter, Capo continued to talk with me, pretending not to notice the movement of the Kraut, who inched his way to the open barn door, and when the Kraut turned very quickly to make a headlong dash to freedom, he found himself in the promised land, for Capo's rifle barked very angrily and spit out a piece of steel that struck the Heiney square between the shoulder blades.

He fell headlong at the feet of old John Rice, who did not even move. He just watched him as his face buried into the manure on the floor at his feet. That little Capo was one more little son-of a-bitch, but a hell of a good man to have on your side. Back in the States a Pole by the name of Benjamin Kolodzieski had hung the name of "Gestapo Charlie" on the little Cuban, but he didn't like the handle worth a damn and would fly off the handle when you called him by that nickname.

But as I watched his action there in front of the barn, I didn't wonder why Kolodzieski hung him with the misnomer of Gestapo Charlie. He had watched the Kraut moving toward the open door for the space of ten minutes, without allowing the Kraut to realize that he was aware of his action. His rifle barrel had been pointed at the Kraut's belly all along, but the Kraut didn't know Gestapo as I knew him. He couldn't read the mischief in his eyes as I could. But now the Kraut lies in a field outside the village, where he serves to fertilize the soil, just like the manure that smeared his face when he fell in the barn. Zeig Heil to Gestapo Charlie!

I left Capo to his mischief and started back down the street, looking for the ambulance. But as I reached the end of the barn where the prisoners were standing, their backs to the wall, I noticed a bunch of identification papers and wallets that had been thrown on top of a manure pile by an over eager, trigger-happy jerk, who evidently thought that the prisoners were no more than animals like himself.

A complete disregard for the personal effects of the Krauts didn't prove a goddamn thing, so I called to the prisoners and told them to get their papers for which they were most grateful. When they had gathered all their papers from the manure, I took one of them by the nape of the neck and marched him down the street to the village square. We halted there for a moment while I looked the surrounding buildings over before making a march on the church that housed the sniper and the machine gunner in its steeple.

Being satisfied that the church was the only building that held any Krauts, I took the prisoner by the arm, punching him in the back with my carbine, and started across the square. My theory was that the Krauts in the church steeple would see the plight of their comrade and allow me safe passage across the square. This was, however, one more hell of a screwed-up theory, for before I could get out into the street, those bastards were popping more lead at our feet than I could stand comfortably. I backed the prisoner up like a jackass harnessed to a cart and made it back to the protection of the nearest house around the corner. I could see that the Krauts in the steeple weren't going to shoot their comrade unless I pressed them into action, and this I damn sure wasn't going to do. So, I told the prisoner to go, pointing my finger in the direction of the barn, and walked about halfway with him before I cut him loose on his own.

I turned back in the direction of the square, but now I crossed the street with the idea that I would have to skirt the village in order to get the ambulance I wanted so much for John Rice. When I reached the other side of the square, I ran into a group of men that stood on the corner of the street, looking out into the square at the form of a medic, whom they thought to be wounded. Major Crosby was in front of the men and asked one of them to go fetch the medic.[11]

When the major saw that none of the men was going to attempt

Chapter 12. A Godforsaken Village

to help the man, he started to go himself. He had taken about two steps out into the square before I reached out and grabbed him by the shoulder and snatched him to the safety of the wall that protected us from the view of the Kraut in the steeple. "Major, you can't go out there," I told him. "I'll go myself."

With this I ran across the street to the position of the medic and stopped over him. I stooped down to grab his wrist to see if there was any pulse. I don't know why I reached for his pulse, for I knew that he was a dead man from the instant I looked him in the face.

There is a saying that a dead man tells no tales, but this man's face told me he had given up the ghost some time ago. His eyes were open, but unseeing, and his face was relaxed into a perfect mask of unworried calm. I had gathered these facts in the instant it took me to kneel at his side, but this was the last face of death that I was to look upon in that troubled village. For a bullet from the sniper's rifle tore through my upper chest and smacked into the wall behind me in such haste that the impact loosened sand and sent small pieces of stone from the building to sting me on the back of the neck. Peculiar, how a man could feel each minute particle hitting him when he has just been kicked by a mule. I felt the stone strike the back of my neck and I felt remorse in my guts for not having succeeded in procuring the ambulance for John Rice.

The impact of the bullet turned me completely around but didn't knock me down. I leaped to my feet and ran across the street, blood spouting from my mouth, and fell at the major's feet. He quickly tore my shirt from my body and turned me on my stomach, pouring sulfathiazole powder in the gaping wound, then bandaged the wound as well as could be managed. When he was satisfied that he could do no more, he took off down the street in a dead run, saying nothing. In just a few minutes a light tank came down the street to stop a few yards from where I lay, still spouting blood from the mouth like an artesian well.[12]

The major jumped out of the top hatch and grabbed me under the arms and hoisted me to my feet. The assistant driver had dismounted and the two of them lifted me to the right hatch and lowered me into the bog's seat.

Two wounded soldiers are loaded onto the rear deck of a M5 light tank (U.S. Army photograph).

Then the major barked a bunch of rapid and very distinct orders to the driver and the gunner. The tank bounded across the square with cannon and machine gun raking both sides of the street. The major was putting the tank right through the middle of the western section of the village, and there were Krauts on both sides of the street. I just suppose the major got a little pissed off because he didn't bother to skirt the town as I had planned when in search for the ambulance for John Rice. John Rice.... Who would help him now? John Rice, my friend.

The tank rumbled across a stream at the edge of town.[13] The Krauts had knocked the bridge out. We struck the main road, and the driver followed the major's orders and poured the coal to the furnace. The light tank bounced up the road at fifty miles per hour, while I sat

Chapter 12. A Godforsaken Village

in the assistant driver's seat, wondering if he was going fast enough to beat the graves registration boys to my carcass.

Sixteen miles to the rear the tank came to a halt in front of the battalion first aid station. The major jumped to the open hatch over my head and lifted me out of the bog's seat, letting me down into the arms of the red headed major doctor, who had been of prior service to me while curing my "cold" which was so prone to run.

This was the last I was to see of Major Crosby, but bless his hide wherever he may be, for had he not taken it upon himself to gather my bones into the tank and hustle me to the first aid station, where the red headed major doctor stopped the bleeding, I would be very dead as far as the body is concerned.

I was sent to a field hospital about thirty miles further to the rear. There I gave the doctor who operated on me a German pistol, the one I used to shoot Blackie in the leg. After the operation they put me in a cot beside a German lieutenant, who had been boogered up the day before, and I found sleep. But John Rice, where was he? I couldn't overcome my concern for John.

When I awoke, I engaged the German lieutenant in conversation as best as could be managed in his broken English. After some time had been spent in talking with him, he said to me, "You're a good man, sergeant."

I wasn't pissed off at him or any of his comrades. I just had to kick them in the creek whenever it became necessary. They loaded me on a hospital train after a week in the field hospital, and took me further to the rear, where they deposited me in a corps hospital. They started punching me in the arm with penicillin every two hours. They kept up this routine until my arms were black and blue, and so sore I couldn't stand the touch of the needle. So, I asked them to try shooting me in the hip. The nurse tried, but I was so flinchy I could not stand her fooling around with my hind quarter. I continued to take it in the arm until they loaded me on another train and took me to Paris.

The train trip was long, and I had ample time to chew my own ass out about John Rice. I envisioned him lying in the barn, dead from loss of blood, because I hadn't gotten him that ambulance. Two

German prisoners took me on a stretcher when we reached the hospital in Paris. They carried me up four flights of stairs and deposited me in a bed next to old long nosed John Rice.[14] *Son-of-a-bitch*, I thought to myself. *I thought the bastard was dead.*

Epilogue

Paris wasn't the last stop on Paul Porter's road to recovery. Three more hospital stays awaited him: England, then New York, and finally, LaGarde General Hospital, a 1650-bed military hospital situated on the south shore of Lake Pontchartrain in New Orleans.[1] On his discharge papers, the description of his wound, "Gun shot wound traversing right side of upper chest," reflected what he described in his memoir.

What Paul *didn't* mention in his manuscript was the recognition he received for his actions on December 4, 1944. On January 30, 1945, while Paul remained hospitalized, a general order letter issued by command of Lieutenant General Patton announced that he had been awarded the Distinguished Service Cross. The order read, in part:

> Sergeant PAUL PORTER, 38494989, Company "B," 53rd Armored Infantry Battalion, 4th Armored Division, United States Army. For extraordinary heroism in connection with military operations against an armed enemy. On December 4 1944 during action to capture the town of DOMFESSEL, FRANCE, Sergeant PORTER distinguished himself by repeated acts of heroism. Completely disregarding his own safety he fought his way through the town, fearlessly engaging the enemy in hand to hand combat wherever he encountered them. Sergeant PORTER was severely wounded while bravely attempting to rescue a wounded medical aid man. His unselfish courage, exemplary heroism and supreme devotion to duty are in keeping with the highest traditions of military service.[2]

On February 25, 1945, Sergeant Porter was on his way back to the USA. He arrived in New York on March 12 and entered a hospital there.[3] He was later transferred to the hospital in New Orleans, the city where he was inducted into the Army just shy of two years earlier.

Epilogue

Left and above: The Company B, 53rd Armored Infantry Battalion Morning Report for December 12, 1944

On April 21, 1945, Paul Porter was honorably discharged with a certificate of disability. He weighed 181 pounds, one pound more than when he entered the Army. That may have been the *only* thing that hadn't changed in two years.[4] His discharge papers noted that, in addition to the Distinguished Service Cross, he received the EMEA[5] Theatre Medal with three Bronze Stars, the Good Conduct Medal, the Purple Heart with Oak Leaf Cluster, and two Overseas Service Bars.[6] His campaign ribbons recognized his participation in the Normandy, Northern France, and German campaigns. He received the coveted Combat Infantryman Badge on August 12, 1944.[7]

Epilogue

After his release from the hospital, Paul remained in the New Orleans area. At first, he wandered the French Quarter. One day, as he walked past a dapper, middle-aged gentleman on the sidewalk, the stranger asked him for a light. Paul Porter had a much more pressing need than did 40-year-old Glenn Charles Palmer. Paul didn't have a home. He asked Glenn if he had a place where he could go. Glenn opened his home to the young war hero, and 728 St. Louis Street became Paul's first known address at the time of his separation from the Army.[8]

Glenn Palmer's residence was less than a half-block from the heart of Bourbon Street. He was born in Arkansas and spent many of his adult years living with his aunt and uncle in St. Louis. He was an openly gay man, which was not typical of the era but perhaps more readily accepted in the heart of New Orleans.[9] Palmer had worked as a shoe salesman since at least 1930 and had arrived in New Orleans sometime after 1940.[10] While in St. Louis, he worked at the Allen Shoe Company. After arriving in New Orleans, he managed their store on Canal Street.[11]

Glenn gave Paul more than a place to live; he gave him a job as well. He also employed Paul's love interest, Joyce Anna Martin.

Like Paul, Joyce was no stranger to family tragedy. When she was 14 years old, her father, Christian Martin, passed away at the age of 48. Joyce was born on May 13, 1927, and New Orleans was the only home she knew. Now, at the tender age of 18, the soldier she fell in love with before he went to war was back at her side. What she didn't know was just how much the war had changed him.

Or had it? Her time with Paul before he shipped off for Europe must have been short (we don't know if they spent time together while he was in training at Camp Bowie). Certainly, she recognized the striking pose he presented when in uniform; he was a man even more dashing when wearing a suit. He was the definition of handsome, complemented by a mischievous and carefree personality. The war hadn't taken those qualities from him.

What Joyce might not have had time to recognize was Paul's restlessness. He was a drifter. A loner. A hustler. Perhaps some of those attributes came from being the last of nine children growing

Epilogue

up during the Great Depression; a situation made even more difficult when, at the age of only six, his mother passed away. He carried some of those qualities onto the battlefield, and perhaps he was alive because of it. But there is little doubt that his experiences in war fertilized his less admirable qualities. And like so many other veterans from his generation, alcohol became his salve. It was a weakness that Joyce would discover soon enough.

On November 11, 1945, Paul and Joyce married in New Orleans. It was not a marriage embraced by Joyce's family. In the absence of

Pictured at the Porter wedding on November 11, 1945; from left: Ruth Blessing; Vic Cerice; William Porter, Sr. (Paul's father); Paul Porter; Joyce Porter; and Joyce's mother, Cecilia Cook Martin (Colleen C. Porter family collection).

Epilogue

a father to vet the potential groom, it was left to her mother Cecilia and other women within Joyce's family circle to protect her interests. They had already witnessed the effects of Paul's use of alcohol and tried without success to head the marriage off at the pass. Their instincts were reinforced as early as the couple's honeymoon. The newlyweds stayed close to home, taking a room at the Cornstalk Hotel. That night, Paul "was in very bar in the Quarter."[12]

The newlyweds went on to enjoy life in the Big Easy. Paul and Joyce made a striking couple when dressed to the nines. They frequented the bars and restaurants of the French Quarter, often in the company of fast friends. Photographs from that time show a happy couple appearing to have the time of their lives. Once married, they moved in with Joyce's mother at 3847 Airline Highway in New Orleans.

Paul and Joyce Porter cutting the cake at their wedding in New Orleans on Sunday, November 11, 1945 (Colleen C. Porter family collection).

The newlyweds continued to work at the shoe store. Paul displayed the flirtatious side of his personality that had, at least from his perspective, served him well during his dash across France in the summer of 1944. One of Joyce's co-workers was a close friend of hers. Paul later admitted, with perhaps a bit of that Porter mischief at the corners of his lips, that when Laura ascended a ladder to retrieve a pair of shoes, he would flirt, saying "you sure have good looking legs, Scully." Despite the overtures, Laura and Joyce remained friends for decades.

Epilogue

There were positive moments in Paul's life as well; he did not live in a sea of total despair. His status was that of a genuine war hero, and during those immediate postwar months, it earned a high level of respect and admiration. His celebrity was heightened on February 18, 1946, when Colonel Sam H. Baker presented him the Distinguished Service Cross. The ceremony took place at the Retreat Parade, Camp Plauche, Louisiana.[13]

Exactly one week following the ceremony, U.S. Congressman James H. Morrison, representing the 6th District of Louisiana, wrote a letter to Paul. After

Glenn Palmer (left) remained a close friend of the Porter family until his death in 1958. This photograph was taken on the day of Paul and Joyce's wedding (Colleen C. Porter family collection).

offering words of congratulation, he wrote, *"You may be assured that your achievement will not be forgotten by the people of the nation for which you bravely fought."*

At some point afterward, Paul underscored in ink the words of Congressman Morrison. His marks upon the page were a sign that disillusionment had set in. Through his underscoring, Paul left the distinct impression that his nation had let him and his fellow veterans down. Lest there be doubt about his sentiment, he later wrote, in stark red ink with an arrow pointing to the Congressman's words, "IS THIS TRUE, OR FALSE?"

Epilogue

A night out on the town in New Orleans. From left to right, Les Skiles, unknown, Joyce Porter, Glenn Palmer, Paul Porter, unknown (Colleen C. Porter family collection).

From left: Paul Porter, his wife Joyce, and his brother William. This postwar photograph was likely taken in New Orleans (Colleen C. Porter family collection).

Epilogue

Colonel Sam H. Baker shakes the hand of Sergeant Paul Porter after bestowing the Distinguished Service Cross (Colleen C. Porter family collection).

In 1950, the Porters welcomed a son, Paul Jr. Remaining close to the Porters, Glenn Palmer was named Paul's godfather. Their daughter Colleen was born in 1953.

Paul eventually left his job at the Allen Shoe Company and settled in as a car salesman for Patterson Pontiac. He never moved his family from his mother-in-law's home and spent much of his time out of the house. Though Paul was often absent from the home, Colleen collected a trove of fond memories of him while she was a young child. Her father loved to barbecue in a home-made pit. He trained homing pigeons and built a bee house. He planted pecan, pear, and apple trees. He doted over Colleen in the backyard, crafting a wooden pair of stilts and teaching her how to use them. He taught her to play the harmonica, mastering the chords and melody to *Red River Valley* and *Bridge Over the River Kwai* (she would play the melody as he accompanied with the chords, and then they would switch parts).

The family's vinyl record player got a lot of use and along with her father's encouragement, it sparked Colleen's interest in music (she eventually became a professional vocalist and composer). He comforted her and held her close when she was sad; it would be years before she understood the nature of the scar that blemished his chest, or the evidence of the exit wound near his shoulder blade.

Paul drew his own comfort from his faith. While he was openly critical of the Catholic Church, he was a student of the Bible and often preached to his family. He admired the work of theologian Emanuel Swedenborg. In later years, he put many of his own thoughts in writing.[14]

Sergeant Porter's wife stands at his side after his receipt of the Distinguished Service Cross (Colleen C. Porter family collection).

Over time, the Porter children saw the dark side of their father's personality. Paul's drinking had a significant impact on the family. On Friday and Saturday nights, he would routinely "get bombed." In anticipation of the difficult weekend ahead, Colleen was sent to a cousin's home for Fridays and Saturdays and then spent Sundays with Laura Scully, her mother's close friend and co-worker with, as

Paul would have reminded us, the "good looking legs."

Drinking can bring out the worst in people. The specter of violence at the Porter home was real and Joyce went to lengths to shield her children from it. More than one plate of food was launched against a wall. Colleen recalled her mother being so frightened that she left the home with her two young children and hid behind a neighboring building.[15] On another occasion, Colleen's Great Aunt Carrie threatened at the point of a gun to rein Paul in. Though he escaped bodily harm at the hands of Aunt Carrie, he wasn't as fortunate when he drove his car through a fence lining a cemetery in New Orleans. He overturned the vehicle on a grave and ended up in the hospital; his brother and a friend snuck him out.[16]

Paul Porter embraces his daughter, Colleen, and son, Paul Jr. (Colleen C. Porter family collection).

The only known attempt to remedy his illness resulted in his commitment to a Veteran's hospital in Biloxi, Mississippi. During his stay, he managed to escape the facility and attempted to hitchhike toward parts unknown. He ended up back in Metairie.[17]

Glenn Palmer also tried to help. He remained close to the Porter family for many years (Colleen recalled Mr. Palmer bringing antique Dutch dolls to their home as a gift). Glenn was sympathetic to the hardships Joyce endured as Paul's wife. According to Colleen, while Glenn was on his death bed in 1958, "he begged mom to leave dad, saying he'll never change."[18]

Perhaps two or three years after Glenn passed, his desire for

Epilogue

Joyce was fulfilled, but not in a manner he would have wished upon the family. Paul's behavior crossed the line in such a way that it was no longer in the family's best interest for him to remain in the household. He had to go.

After Paul left the family home, his travels are not easily traced. He favored the West, and his known residences over the years were in California, Washington, and Alaska. On at least one occasion that we know of, he ventured out of that geographic box to spend time in Cuba with a friend by the name of Albert Mince.[19] At some point, Paul's adult son and second wife joined him in

Paul Porter outside of the Patterson Pontiac car dealership in New Orleans, where he held a sales position following his employment with the Allen Shoe Company (Colleen C. Porter family collection).

San Francisco, where they all stayed with Paul's sister Doris. In Colleen's words, "Dad and brother hung out." During his time with his son, they traveled to the vicinity of Mount Shasta and took several pictures with the beautiful, snow-covered peak behind them.[20]

A small pension provided some income and he managed to send money to his family in New Orleans monthly. As Colleen said, "It was not much."[21] It is not clear by what other means he supported himself over the years. Though Paul had left his family, he had not abandoned them; they seemed to remain in his mind and in his heart. He wrote often to his estranged wife and daughter.

Though he drifted, the winds carried him back to New Orleans

Epilogue

every year or so. His arrival in Louisiana was often preceded by a series of post cards or letters sent from increasingly closer locales; the cancelled postage stamps offered clues about his route. When he arrived, he always brought stories with him.

Once Dad drives across the Bay Saint Louis bridge in Mississippi. He sees 2 men fishing. Dad stops the car, gets out and shouts, "I'm with Fish and Gaming" and flashes his wallet. Dad takes the fishing poles and drives off.[22]

In 1965, Joyce filed for a formal separation from Paul. The proceedings ended in her favor, and she was granted sole custody of her two children. As part of the judge's ruling, Paul was forbidden from "molesting, interfering, harassing his wife, JOYCE MARTIN PORTER, or from attempting to take away the minor children."[23]

It was perhaps at this time that Paul started writing his combat memoir.[24] We know that in 1967, the manuscript made its way to a literary agent in New York City. The submission to the agent was made by Ed Hicks of Fort Smith, Arkansas, who wrote a compelling case for a review of the manuscript. The ball was in Paul's court to follow up on it.[25]

He never did. Sometime later, Paul attached a hand-written note to Hick's letter, confessing "Never did I get around to sending the manuscript to this man—I know not why."

After Colleen entered adulthood, Paul regularly found his way back to her. Some of his appearances were anticipated while others came out of the blue. No matter the events of the past, Colleen welcomed each visit, hoping beyond hope that alcohol would not poison the experience. At every turn, she was disappointed. She described one such occasion that took place during the mid–1970s:

> I was living in Houston Texas singing. Dad arrived at my door unannounced! He's standing there outside my door dressed in black and a cowboy hat and cowboy boots. He was drinking out of a bottle wrapped in a brown paper bag. He had a cab driver with him. He says, "Come in, this is my kid's place." I said, "I'll take the package, does he owe you (the cab driver) any money?" The man says no. I said, "Let's go get you some food. But if you drink, I'm leaving you there. Ok?" He says ok. While I'm driving, he says, "stop, I need cigarettes." He goes into a food store and comes out with beer, so I leave him there!

Epilogue

She relished the minutes of the day during his visit when his demons took a rest. But eventually, his drinking tipped the scale to the point that she had all that she could stand. She always held out hope that the next time would be different; just a little improvement would be enough. Sadly, a little bit never came, but her hope never subsided.

On May 19, 1974, tragedy struck yet again for the Porter family. A 51-year-old man entered the city landfill in the town of Terrell, Texas. He was divorced and was carving out a living as a carpenter. Cradled in his arms was a shotgun. He turned it on himself and blew his brains out. It was Paul's fraternal twin brother, Silas.[26]

During the late 1970s, Paul's interest in the manuscript was reignited. In October of 1978, he paid a literary agent a reading fee of $150.[27] We don't know what the response was to his work, other than the fact that it was not published. The pages yellowed with the passage of time.

Paul continued to show signs of bitterness over his plight. He believed, or perhaps feared, that the sacrifices made by his generation were being ignored. On the final page of a copy of his typed manuscript, 34 years after the war and 11 years after writing his memoir, he placed a handwritten entry that once again harkened back to the words of

Fraternal twins Silas (left) and Paul Porter (right) (Colleen C. Porter family collection).

Epilogue

Congressman Morrison: *"Is it like the Congressman said? Have we been forgotten?"* His doubts also extended to his ex-wife and daughter. On the back of a photograph, he wrote, *"How come you guys don't write? Are you also turned against me? Your father, Paul."*

While Paul's demons proved to be too strong, his family, and especially his daughter, saw flashes of the down-to-earth little boy from Oklahoma. He continued to tell stories about his antics ... none of which were done with malice. Had he hurt people? Certainly. Was it ever his intention? No. He was, at heart, a good old boy from Oklahoma. And it was in Oklahoma where he would make his final home, close to the very place where he was born.

Paul died on July 9, 1985, less than three months shy of his 62nd birthday. He lived a hard, difficult, and challenging life, from nearly beginning to end. In death, he rests beside his brother Silas, just as he had in his mother's womb. They are buried in Brushy, not far from the place of his birth.

Engraved on Paul's tombstone is his status as a veteran of World War II along with the recognition of his Distinguished Service Cross. As honorable as that is, the words that may have meant the most to him are not found at his grave. They were uttered 80 years ago by a German officer whose name he never knew: *"You're a good man, Sergeant."*

Chapter Notes

Preface (Porter)

1. Letter from Ed Hicks of Forth Smith, Arkansas to Mr. Scott Meredith of Scott Meredith Literary Agency located in NYC, dated November 28, 1967. Mr. Hicks was presented the manuscript by a third party (Johnie Goines, also of Ft. Smith, Arkansas) on behalf of Porter. Paul's address was identified in the letter as 3826 K Johnson Street, Metairie, Louisiana.

2. Unlike all other divisions in the United States Army, the Fourth Armored Division did not have a nickname (for example, the Second Armored Division is "Hell on Wheels," and the Third Armored Division is "Spearhead"). This was the result of Major General Wood's insistence that the Fourth did not require a nickname. Instead, he believed the title Fourth Armored Division was "name enough." When asked to provide a nickname, his response was, "The Fourth Armored Division does not and will not have a nickname. They shall be known by their deeds alone."

Preface (Fox)

1. A section of the manuscript that fell out of sync with official records was Porter's description of the fighting in the vicinity of Berg during late November and the first days of December 1944. During this period, the 53rd Armored Infantry Battalion fought through a series of small towns (e.g., Kirrberg, Postroff, Baerendorf, Eschwiller, Eywiller, Berg, and Rimsdorf). Porter appears to have conflated some of the events during this stretch of time.

2. The individual battalion KIA data is drawn from the book *Our Blood and His Guts*, by Eugene W. Luciano, a veteran of the 10th Armored Infantry Battalion. In Luciano's work, the name of every member of the division killed in action is listed by unit at the battalion level.

3. Koyen, Kenneth. *The Fourth Armored Division from the Beach to Bavaria.*

4. Bellanger, Yves J. *U.S. Army Armored Division 1943–1945 Organization, Doctrine, Equipment.*

5. Major General John S. Wood was arguably the most capable commander of armor for the U.S. Army during World War II. Wood graduated from the United States Military Academy at West Point in 1912. His time at West Point overlapped future leaders including Dwight D. Eisenhower, Omar Bradley, Jacob Devers, Carl Spaatz, William Simpson, and George Patton. In Patton, he found a life-long friend. Wood was a veteran of the First World War, having risen to the rank of major and serving as the ordnance officer for the 3rd Division. Like many in the military, his career stalled during the two decades following the Great War. As the United States ramped up for war once again, opportunities came his way, and during the spring of 1941, he replaced Major General Henry Welles Baird as the commanding general of the Fourth Armored Division. Wood's emphasis on training was legendary, which led to the division's superb performance in combat. He also spawned great talent, the most famous being General Creighton Abrams, who would eventually become the Army Chief of Staff.

Notes—Introduction

As for Wood, despite his superb performance, he was relieved of his command by Patton on December 2 or 3, 1944, just prior to Sergeant Porter's final day of battle. Wood was sent back to the United States to command the Armored Replacement Center at Fort Knox, Kentucky. The assignment was a bitter pill for him to swallow. A thorough account of Patton's relief of Wood may be found in *Patton's Vanguard—The United States Army Fourth Armored Division*. John S. Wood died on July 2, 1966, at the age of 78.

6. Fox, Don M. *Patton's Vanguard—The United States Army Fourth Armored Division*.

Introduction

1. Paul's siblings were Ethel (1909–1938), Ella Mae (1911–1960), Bessie (1913–1919), Pollie (1915–1952), Doris Dean (1917–1980), William Monroe (1919–1986), John B (1921–1998), and Silas Oscar (1923–1974).

2. Marriage records for Sequoyah County, Oklahoma, 1907–09, page 212.

3. The 1910 census lists William Porter's occupation as a home farmer; the family residence was in Sadie Township, Oklahoma. His World War I draft registration reflects farmer, as does the 1920 census.

4. Later in life, Paul told his daughter stories of living in a home with dirt floors.

5. The estimated annual income in 2023 dollars is approximately $11,000.

6. 1940 U.S. Census data. All indications are that during his youth, Paul worked on the farms his family was associated with.

7. *Santa Maria Times*, November 17, 1941. The front-page news story appeared below the fold and carried the headline *Santa Maria Sends Out Its Biggest "Draft Order."*

8. The draft registration card for John B. Porter. In 1951, John married Betty Antoinette Bianchini. He passed away on November 29, 1998, in Cottonwood, Arizona. He was buried in Brushy, Oklahoma.

9. The draft registration card for William Porter, Sr. (required even at his age of 56).

10. Paul Porter's draft registration card.

11. The Porter family possesses several photographs taken of Paul during his time in the Army (most likely all taken before going overseas) that he sent or gave (likely mailed) to Joyce with heartfelt inscriptions, thus leading us to believe that the two met prior to Paul going overseas. Most likely, they met during the brief time he would have been in New Orleans for induction. Unfortunately, details beyond that are unknown.

12. Fox, Don M. *Patton's Vanguard—The United States Army Fourth Armored Division*, page 19.

13. By the time the war ended, Lt. Col. George L. Jaques had the distinction of being the only one of the commanding officers of the three armored infantry battalions to remain in command during the entire campaign. Lieutenant Colonels Graham Kirkpatrick and Arthur West of the 10th Armored Infantry Battalion were both wounded in action; Lt. Col. Harold Cohen was the last commander of the 10th AIB in combat. The 51st Armored Infantry Battalion lost two commanding officers as well: Lt. Col. Alfred Maybach was killed in action and his successor, Major Harry Van Arnam, wounded in action. Lt. Col. Dan Alanis commanded the battalion until the end of the war. Like many others from the Fourth Armored Division, Jaques hailed from the northeast region of the United States. "Jigger Jakes," as he later became known by his fellow soldiers, was born May 31, 1910, in Fitchburg, Massachusetts. Unlike many peers of his rank, he retired after his service in World War II (though he remained in the Active Reserves until 1957 with the rank of colonel). He carved out a successful business career, serving in the roles of vice president, production manager and purchasing agent for Judson Dunaway Corp. in Dover, New Hampshire. His last career position was president (or vice-president) of D'Arcy Millwork in Dover. He also served as a director of Capitol Products

Notes—Chapter 1

Aluminum Company of New England. He died at the age of 51 on July 18, 1961, following surgery in Boston.

14. 53rd AIB Unit Diary entry for September 10, 1943.

15. Yves J. Bellanger. *U.S. Army Armored Division 1943–1945 Organization, Doctrine, Equipment*, pages 267–8.

16. 53rd AIB Unit Diary entry for December 29, 1943. The USAT Santa Paula was a passenger ocean liner constructed in 1932 for the Grace Line. When converted for wartime service, she could transport approximately 2,200 troops. Enlisted men slept in bunks stacked four to six high. During her four years of wartime service, she completed 28 overseas voyages (source: *Troopships of World War II* by Roland W. Charles, published by the Army Transport Association, Washington, D.C., 1947).

17. 53rd AIB Unit Diary entry for February 3, 1944.

18. 53rd AIB Unit Diary entry for March 3, 1944.

19. Modern day satellite imagery shows the pockmarked landscape that is still employed today for live fire maneuvers. The general area is known as Salisbury Plain and was used extensively by the Fourth Armored Division and many other units as they continued their training before being committed to combat.

20. 53rd AIB Unit Diary entry for May 10, 1944.

Chapter 1

1. According to the 53rd AIB Unit Diary, Company B embarked at the Port of Weymouth on July 12. They debarked at Utah Beach on July 14 and proceeded to their bivouac area 5.5 miles southeast of Barneville. In Porter's original manuscript, he noted July 17 as the date of arrival. This has been corrected to avoid confusion regarding the timeline.

2. Steve J. Cardone served with the Fourth Armored Division since the training period at Pine Camp, NY. His name and photo appear in the book for the 51st Armored Infantry Regiment. He was a private assigned to Company B and was later promoted to sergeant. Cardone, along with six other enlisted men (including Pfc. J.P. Doss), was listed as slightly sick and transferred to a hospital as a non-battle casualty on November 27. During the month of November, he was also treated for a shoulder wound received as the result of artillery fire. Cardone was born on January 2, 1912, in the Bronx, New York. He registered for the draft on October 16, 1940, while employed as a custodian by the board of education. At the time of his enlistment on March 18, 1942, he worked as a fireman. His discharge date was November 19, 1945, by which time he had achieved the rank of staff sergeant. He died on September 14, 1976, and was buried at St. Raymond's in the Bronx.

3. A "section 8" refers to a military discharge for issues relating to mental illness or undesirable traits of behavior or character. During World War II, the applicable code was found in Section VIII, Army Regulation 615–360.

4. Porter's paraphrasing of Confucius was likely related to the Chinese philosopher's saying, "To lead uninstructed people to war is to throw them away."

5. Lt. Gen. Omar Bradley chose the Fourth Armored Division for this assignment, much to the disgust of Major General Wood, who firmly believed that his division had been trained for the purpose of offensive action and exploitation. In his opinion, placing his valuable armored infantrymen into a static role in relief of the 4th Infantry Division was a terrible waste of his men. He had a heated debate with Bradley before reluctantly carrying out the order. It was Wood's nature to speak his mind when he disagreed; a trait that would eventually lead to him being relieved of his command. Combat Command B, led by Brigadier Holmes B. Dager, was chosen to execute the mission of replacing the elements of the 4th Infantry Division in the line. CCB was assigned all three of the Fourth's armored infantry battalions (the 10th, 51st, and 53rd), all of the armored field artillery battalions (the 22nd, 66th, and 94th), the 704th Tank Destroyer Battalion, two troops of the 25th Armored Cavalry Reconnaissance Squadron, and

Notes—Chapter 2

service echelons (*4th Armored Division Combat History*, entry for July 17). The company that Porter's Company B relieved was part of the 4th Infantry Division's 8th Infantry Regiment. The position they took over was approximately five miles south-southeast of the village of Baupte.

6. The front line at that point was approximately 12 miles south-southeast of Utah beach.

7. The 4th Infantry Division participated in the D-Day invasion with responsibility for securing Utah Beach. After playing a key role in the capture of Cherbourg (an operation in which they lost 5,400 men), they reentered the line with an abundance of replacement troops. Now under the control of VII Corps, their losses continued to mount. On July 7 alone, they suffered almost 600 casualties (Blumenson, *Breakout and Pursuit*).

8. Opposing the Fourth Armored Division in this sector were elements of the *2nd SS Panzer Division* (*3rd Battalion, 3rd SS Regiment*) and *2nd and 3rd Battalions, 6th Para Regiment* (Fourth A.D. combat history entry for July 18).

9. "Little Corporal" was a pejorative nickname for Adolph Hitler. It was based upon the rank he held during the First World War.

Chapter 2

1. T/Sergeant Michael J. Kelly appears on the morning report for December 4, 1944. He was transferred to a hospital as of November 24, 1944, listed as slightly sick and a non-battle casualty, and dropped from assignment.

2. Lt. John W. Luxbacher is first mentioned in the 53rd AIB Unit Diary on February 9, 1944, while the battalion was in England. Luxbacher was born August 1, 1918, in Pennsylvania. He grew up in Beadling and was inducted on March 12, 1941, in Pittsburgh. Luxbacher completed high school, and prior to his service, worked as an electric assembler for a hearing aid factory. At the time he registered for the draft, he worked for Conte-Eastwood Construction. He continued to serve after World War II, including service in Korea. By the end of his military career, he achieved the rank of major. Luxbacher died March 30, 1989.

3. George Joseph Wanosik was born May 17, 1925, in Dennison, Ohio. His father (John) was born in Czechoslovakia (John's obituary appeared in The Daily Reporter, July 16, 1963). George completed two years of high school and then registered for the draft on June 17, 1943; he enlisted four days later. On December 12, 1944, he was appointed to the rank of staff sergeant. On December 14 he received a certificate of merit. On December 24, during the Battle of the Bulge, he was wounded in the chest by artillery shell fragments while engaged in combat near the village of Bigonville. He was evacuated and released from treatment during January 1945. He received the Silver Star and Purple Heart. Wanosik died February 10, 1990.

4. 2nd Lieutenant James Duffy, Jr., is first mentioned in the battalion diary on June 18, when he departed for London to participate in a one-week instruction on street fighting. Accompanying him were Lt. Harold E. Watts, T/Sgt. Roy Mitchell (later KIA), and S/Sgt. Ivan D. Green. Lt. Duffy's death is noted in the battalion diary on July 18. *"2nd Lt. James Duffy was the first to be killed in action. He was killed while inspecting his patrols on the front lines."* The Fourth Armored Division combat history entry for July 18 also states, *"it is believed he was killed by his own men as he passed through their line of fire."* A native of Michigan, Lt. Duffy is interred at the Normandy cemetery in St. Laurent, France (block C, row 26, grave 22).

5. Captain Francis J. O'Brien is first mentioned in the battalion diary on April 25, 1944. On that date, he was assigned the role of battalion S-3 for the purpose of a special exercise. According to the battalion morning report for September 22, Captain O'Brien was transferred from Company B to HQ 4th Armored Division Trains effective September 21. (This after having returned to the battalion on September 16 after having been lightly wounded in action.) O'Brien served with the Fourth Armored Division since the time of training at Pine

Notes—Chapter 3

Camp; his name and photo appear in the book for the 51st Armored Infantry Regiment. His rank at the time was 1st lieutenant and he was assigned to Company B of the 1st Battalion.

6. Porter joined the Fourth Armored while the division trained at Camp Bowie, Texas.

7. Private J. P. Doss appears on the morning report for December 5, 1944. At that time, it was indicated that as of November 27, 1944, he was slightly sick and transferred to a hospital. He had been previously wounded in the thigh by artillery fire during September. Doss was born in 1921 in Tennessee and his education did not extend beyond grammar school. He worked on a farm and enlisted on October 15, 1942, in Louisville, Kentucky.

8. The M1 carbine, when fully loaded, weighed under six pounds. The M1 Garand semi-automatic rifle was a heavier weapon (approximately 10 pounds) and considerably more powerful. Given Porter's role on the light machine gun squad, it is not surprising that he favored the lighter weapon.

Chapter 3

1. Pfc. Konsicky's name is not found among the list of men KIA from the 53rd AIB. There is a Pfc. Joseph Klinkosky who served in the 53rd AIB and was KIA; Porter likely misremembered his name.

2. Private John Kovacs served with the Fourth Armored Division since training at Pine Camp. His name and photo appear in the book for the 51st Armored Infantry Regiment as a member of Company B. His hometown was Middlesex, New Jersey. He had completed four years of high school before his enlistment date of May 15, 1941. He entered the service at Trenton, New Jersey. During the month of September 1944, he was wounded in the leg by artillery fire. The morning report for December 12, 1944, indicates that he was slightly sick and transferred to a hospital on December 6, 1944, and dropped from assignment.

3. First Sergeant Arnold Wuestenhagen is first mentioned in the battalion diary on April 9, 1944, when he "left to attend a six day Documents Indoctrination Course in London, England." The diary states he was with Company B at that time. He appears on the Company B morning report for September 13; he had been transferred to the 39th Evacuation Hospital as of September 8 and listed as "slightly sick non-battle casualty dropped from assignment." He had served with the Fourth Armored Division since the training days at Pine Camp; his name and photograph appear in the book produced by the division in 1942. In that publication, he is listed as serving in the Headquarters Company of the 1st Battalion, 51st Armored Infantry Regiment. Wuestenhagen was one of the seasoned men of the division. Born on May 30, 1905, in Sheboygan, Wisconsin, his father Fred immigrated to the United States in 1883 from Germany. Arnold was the second oldest of eight children. At the age of 14, he worked in a toy factory in Sheboygan. As of the 1940 census, he was married to his wife Carmen and was stationed at Jefferson Barracks in St. Louis, Missouri, having achieved the rank of sergeant. He died from suffocation on February 8, 1973, while in Guadalajara, Mexico (*Report of Death of American Citizens Abroad*).

4. The 53rd Armored Infantry Battalion suffered significant casualties and was disorganized after the German attack, with many members of the battalion fleeing the front line. The 10th Armored Infantry Battalion was given command of the front and restored the situation. As noted in the 53rd AIB Unit Diary, the battalion was reorganized approximately 5 miles to the rear on July 19. At 2000 hours, the battalion moved closer to the front into a reserve position, where they remained until July 27.

5. On February 3, 1944, while in England, the entire battalion was assembled at the Garrison Theatre to hear a lecture given by the First Army pre-capture team. The topic was "What to Do in the Event of Capture" (53rd AIB Unit Diary).

6. In Porter's original manuscript, he identified the battalion as belonging to the 29th Infantry Division. This was an

error; the 29th was not in the vicinity at that time. The battalion in question is not certain.

7. This was the beginning of Operation Cobra, which led to the breakout from Normandy. The actual numbers for the aerial bombardment on July 25 were 1,500 B-17 and B-24 bombers, 380 medium bombers, and 550 fighter-bombers (a total of 2,430 bombers of all types). All did not go as planned when a significant number of bombs fell short of their targets and impacted several American units, wounding 490 and killing 111 including Lt. Gen. Lesley J. McNair, the commanding general of the Army Ground Forces (Blumenson, *Breakout and Pursuit*, pages 234–6). These casualties came on top of an aborted attempt at launching Cobra the day prior. The aerial bombardment on July 24 was called off due to poor weather conditions, but not all of the aircraft received the recall order. A number of bombs fell short that day as well, killing 25 and wounding 131 members of the 30th Infantry Division (Blumenson, *Breakout and Pursuit*, page 229).

8. Following the opening air bombardment, VII Corps of the U.S. First Army initiated the primary ground attack at 1100 hours on July 25. The operational plan called for the infantry divisions of VII Corps to make the initial thrust through the (hopefully) shattered German line; the Third and Second Armored Divisions would continue the advance to the southwest with the objective of trapping the German units facing VIII Corps (Blumenson, *Breakout and Pursuit*). The Fourth Armored Division was assigned to VIII Corps and would remain in place until the VII Corps attack had progressed. Combat Command B would lead the advance for the Fourth Armored. The 53rd AIB, attached to Combat Command B, began its advance at 0500 hours on July 28 (Fourth Armored unit history and 53rd AIB Unit Diary).

Chapter 4

1. The original plan was for the Sixth Armored Division to secure Avranches while the Fourth Armored protected the east flank of the advance. When the Sixth AD's advance stalled, the Fourth Armored was give the mission of capturing Avranches and leading the breakout into Brittany.

2. Properly, the Brittany Peninsula. The port city of Brest is located at the far west end of the Brittany Peninsula.

3. Major General John Shirley Wood was no stranger to the front lines of his division. Not satisfied with the pace of CCB's attack on Coutances, he entered the town on foot under enemy fire and proceeded to capture a German soldier. After navigating a minefield, he sent a hand-written message to the commander of CCB: "General Dager, send the Infantry through after me." Maj. Gen. Wood was awarded the Distinguished Service Cross for his action at Coutances (Fox, *Patton's Vanguard*, page 45).

4. Other elements of the Fourth Armored (including elements of the 53rd AIB) had cleared Coutances prior to the arrival of Company B. The town was mopped up by the end of July 29 (53rd AIB after action report and Blumenson, *Breakout and Pursuit*, page 312).

5. While the *Luftwaffe* did show itself against the Fourth Armored as it advanced toward Avranches, research for this work has failed to find evidence of an attack of this magnitude.

6. The German *7th Army* was in disarray. One of the armored columns of CCB passed within a few hundred yards of the *7th Army* forward command post. Several German officers, including *General* Hausser and *Generalmajor* Rudolf Christeph, made their escape by dashing across the highway during intervals in the CCB column (Fox, *Patton's Vanguard*, page 50).

7. The most well-known encounter between the Fourth Armored Division and Russian units occurred on August 7 when a task force from the 37th Tank Battalion overran the *281st Ost Cavalry Battalion* (Fox, *Patton's Vanguard*, pages 72–73).

8. Private Charles Capo was born in 1919 and enlisted on May 15, 1941, in New York City. He had completed two

Notes—Chapter 5

years of high school and worked as a porter before his enlistment. He served with the Fourth Armored Division as early as the Pine Camp training. His name and photo appear in the Pine Camp book for the 51st Armored Infantry Regiment. He was assigned to Company B, 1st Battalion. On the morning report for December 1, 1944, Capo, who by then had apparently been promoted to sergeant, was listed as lightly wounded in action as of November 24 and transferred to a hospital as a battle casualty. His injuries were on the face and neck and attributed to a land mine while on foot; treatment was "debridement without closure." On the morning report for December 11, it is reported that he returned to duty on December 10 (these dates appear to be at odds with Porter's account). On January 14, 1945, Capo was evacuated to the 35th Evacuation Hospital due to illness (as stated on the morning report for January 16). His medical report indicated a diagnosis of "Pes cavus," which is a foot malady.

9. Joe Kiernan's name appears on the morning report for October 1. Records indicate he was transferred to the 35th Evacuation Hospital as of September 24 as a non-battle casualty slightly sick. He appears again on the morning report for October 26, this time transferred to the 12th Evacuation Hospital effective October 24, again as a slightly sick non battle casualty.

Chapter 5

1. The actual distance (straight line) is approximately 40 miles.

2. The support from the 8th Infantry Division was provided by a regimental combat team of the 13th Infantry Regiment (*Fourth Armored Combat History*, August 2 entry). In Porter's original manuscript, he incorrectly identified the support as coming from the 35th Infantry Division.

3. The "military slope," also known as the "military crest," is the point on a hill or ridge (not the actual crest) where the observation and field of fire extends to the base of the hill (or ridge).

4. Frank Simonazzi, Jr., appears on the Company B morning report for October 29. Effective October 25, he was promoted from Pfc. to Tec 5. As stated on the morning report for December 14, on December 5, he was lightly wounded in action and dropped from assignment. His hospital admission card indicates he was wounded in the leg by artillery shell fragments. Medical treatment was "closure of wound, delayed (suture, secondary to wound) (delayed closure). Simonazzi was born on August 1, 1917, in Blythedale, Pennsylvania. According to the 1920 census, his parents, sister, and two brothers were all born in Italy and last lived in Naples before immigrating to the United States; only he and his older brother Oscar were born in the USA. His education did not extend beyond 8th grade. He registered for the draft on October 16, 1940, and worked at that time for Pittsburgh Coal Company. Based upon the information on his application for World War II compensation, he entered domestic service on December 10, 1941, at Fort Meade, Maryland, and foreign service on December 29, 1943. He reentered domestic service on April 29, 1945. On January 13, 1951, he was granted a marriage license with Margaret Kish, who was 10 years his junior. Margaret's parents were immigrants as well, having come to the USA from Austria-Hungary. Frank died on June 11, 1985, and was buried at Penn Lincoln Memorial Park, in North Huntingdon, Pennsylvania.

5. Porter was certainly referring to the port city of Lorient. The original mission for VIII Corps (to which the Fourth was assigned) was to secure the major ports in Brittany; the Fourth Armored Division had the initial responsibility for Lorient. The pre-invasion plan considered these ports to be vital resources that would support the Allied advance toward Germany. Major General Wood's desire was to continue pressing east into the enemy vitals; he expressed outrage over being sent west. As for Lorient, it became quickly apparent that the Fourth Armored Division was ill-equipped to attack such a heavily defended and dense urban area. Rather than assault the city,

Notes—Chapter 5

elements of Wood's division contained the enemy there for several days before being ordered to move east. As it turned out, the ports were of less value than originally planned, and in the case of Lorient, the enemy was simply contained there until the end of the war (Fox, *Patton's Vanguard*, pages 70–77).

6. The Fourth Armored Division, like most of their peer divisions (the exceptions being the Second and Third Armored Divisions), consisted of three combat commands: A, B, and Reserve (the latter often referred to simply as CCR). According to Army doctrine, CCA and CCB were the two primary fighting commands. The units assigned to them would vary depending upon the mission. Combat Command Reserve, as the name suggests, was a place for units of the division to be placed for rest and refitting, as well as serving as reserves that would rotate into CCA or CCB. Within a combat command, it was common for the units to be assembled into two or more task forces at a time (the formation of two task forces was most common). Within the Fourth Armored Division, the usual practice was to make one of the task forces heavy with armor (e.g., two medium tank companies and one company of armored infantry) while the other favored infantry (two companies of armored infantry and one medium tank company). The tank-heavy task force would usually be commanded by the tank battalion commander or one of his staff officers while the infantry-heavy task force was commanded by the commander of the armored infantry battalion or staff officer. In the Fourth Armored Division, each task force was named for the officer in command (e.g., TF Abrams or TF Jaques). All of the armored divisions followed a similar practice for the formation of task forces, though not all named them after the commanding officers. A unique trait of the Fourth Armored was that it was the only armored division to use CCR in its intended role; the other armored divisions routinely deployed their CCR as a fighting command. The Fourth committed CCR to battle on rare occasions, one of which occurred during the Battle of the Bulge (for greater organizational detail, see Fox, *Patton's Vanguard*—pages 20–26).

7. It is unlikely that the tank was from the 8th Tank Battalion. However, records for the 8th TB are incomplete for this period due to the destruction of the original documents during enemy action. At the same time, records of the 37th TB and 35th TB do not align with attachment to the 53rd AIB.

8. The Lt. Green in question may be 2nd Lieutenant Walter E. Green, who first appears in the 53rd AIB diary on June 11. However, his assignment within the battalion is not indicated. The other (and more likely) possibility is 2nd Lieutenant Ivan D. Green, who is first mentioned in the battalion diary on June 19, 1944. On October 25, 1944, he is recognized in the battalion diary as one of seven members of the battalion awarded the Silver Star and is identified as being from Company B. Also listed from Company B as a Silver Star recipient is T/Sgt. Edward J. McCormack (McCormack would later be promoted to 2nd Lt. and eventually KIA). Members of Company B receiving the Bronze Star that day were Captain Alfred J. Owen, Sgt. Raymond Cooper, and 1st Lt. Robert F. Everson (for Everson, it was an Oak Leaf Cluster). According to the morning report for December 3, 1944, Sgt. Cooper would be lightly wounded in action on November 27, 1944, and transferred to a hospital. Lt. Everson would have the personal fortune of being sent to the United States on detached service as of December 10, 1944, just prior to the Battle of the Bulge.) On the Company B morning report for October 6, it is noted that Ivan Green was promoted from T/Sgt. to 2nd lieutenant effective September 15. The field promotion aligns with Porter's account, but not the timing. On the Company B morning report for December 1, 1944, it was noted that he was lightly wounded in action on November 24 and transferred to a hospital. Green was a long-term member of the battalion, having served during the training period at Pine Camp. A sergeant at that time, his name and photo appear

in the book for the 51st Armored Infantry Regiment.

9. "Sally Goodin" is an old-time fiddler song, especially popular in the part of the country where Porter was raised.

Chapter 6

1. The 53rd AIB reached Blois on August 20, as noted in the battalion diary. On that day, the battalion was assigned to Combat Command Reserve. Company B was given the mission of outposting a 20-mile line along the Loire River from Blois to Beaugency. One platoon (Porter's third platoon) was sent to Blois, and the battalion diary notes, "The platoon at Blois reported small arms fire from the South side of the Loire river throughout the night."

2. Information on the life of John J. Rice has been difficult to find. Through his serial number (33727672) we know that he was born in 1923. He enlisted in the U.S. Army on June 21, 1943. He completed two years of high school, and his civil occupation was "Packing, filling, labeling, marking, bottling, and related occupations."

3. According to the 53rd AIB Unit Diary, the battalion departed the vicinity of Blois on August 24. The battalion records align with Porter's account of enemy fire coming from across the river. The entry for August 25 states that the battalion, then under Combat Command Reserve, departed the vicinity of Saint-Laurent at 0715 hours and traveled 124 miles to the vicinity of Villeneuve-l'Archevêque.

4. While Porter may have been under the impression that Strasbourg was an objective for the Fourth Armored, he was mistaken. There is no telling what rumors may have been circulating at the time.

5. The 53rd AIB was engaged in Troyes on August 26 and 27. The initial attack on the city was executed by CCA; elements of the 10th AIB and 35th Tank Battalion played significant roles and are usually credited with the capture of the city. The 53rd AIB was brought forward to assist and played an important role in securing Troyes. The assault on Troyes earned fame for the Fourth Armored Division based upon their use of a desert formation to cross the open ground west of the city. Lt. Gen. Patton described it as "a very magnificent feat of arms" (Fox, *Patton's Vanguard*—pages 88–93).

6. The Fourth Armored Division's advance was so rapid and unexpected that its units outran their maps. Troyes was a large city and the lack of maps made operations a greater challenge. During the battle, a squad of infantry from the 10th Armored Infantry Battalion accessed a large quantity of maps when they captured a German headquarters that included an elaborate communications center. In addition, the squad took 50 prisoners and seized approximately 500 rifles, carbines, and machine guns, as well as ten trucks and a motorcycle (Fox, *Patton's Vanguard*, page 91).

Chapter 7

1. According to the battalion records, the 53rd AIB departed Troyes at 2030 hours on August 27. They bivouacked for the night only 10 miles northeast of Troyes. They departed at 0700 hours on August 28 and reached the outskirts of Vitry-le-François at 1100 hours. "Companies "A" and "B" crossed the Marne River by wading and seized the high ground north of the town. The battalion (-Co "C") set up a defensive position on the northern outskirts of the town." The battalion remained in this position on August 28 and was subjected to shelling that resulted in only one casualty. On August 30, the battalion engaged the enemy at Villers-en-Lieu. They outposted the town for the night. On August 31, the battalion advance over 30 miles to Commercy on the Meuse River. After crossing the river, they bivouacked two miles north of Vignot. They remained in this area until being relieved by the 80th Infantry Division on September 2. The battalion moved into position on the high ground one mile south of the village of Gironville. The 53rd remained there until the morning of September 11, when it moved into position near the Moselle River.

Notes—Chapter 8

2. The Company B morning report for September 8 indicates that Porter was transferred to the 302nd Evacuation Hospital on September 6. "Slightly sick non battle casualty dropped from assignment." His rank is listed as Pfc. On the morning report for September 11, his rank is corrected to private. This entry also provides his MOS (745) and serial number (38493989). "MOS" is the military occupation code (in other words, the soldier's job assignment). MOS 745 is a rifleman. On the morning report for December 18, 1944, a correction to a prior morning report indicates that Porter returned to duty on September 8, 1944.

3. On September 13, Company B was detached from the 53rd AIB and attached to Task Force Abrams (Lt. Col. Creighton Abrams, commanding officer of the 37th Tank Battalion). After crossing the Moselle, TF Abrams proceeded to wreak havoc deep behind the German lines east of the city of Nancy. Company B was heavily involved in these actions and would return to the 53rd AIB on September 19.

4. Prior to Company B crossing the Moselle, a high-level conference was held on the west side of the river. Major General Wood, Colonel Bruce Clarke (commander of CCA), Major General Manton Eddy (commanding general of XII Corps), Lt. Col. Creighton Abrams (commanding officer of the 37th Tank Battalion), and Major General Horace McBride (commanding general of the 80th Infantry Division) discussed the wisdom of allowing CCA to pass through the bridgehead being tenuously held by the 80th Infantry Division. When Clarke asked Abrams what he thought, Abrams replied, "Colonel, that is the shortest way home." In other words, attacking to the east and eventually into Germany was the best way to make it back to America (Fox, *Patton's Vanguard*, page 114).

5. T/5 Alvin Gross appears on the morning report for December 11, 1944. He was listed as slightly sick and a non-battle casualty transferred to a hospital on November 27, 1944. Gross, who lived in Somerset County, Maine, enlisted on February 5, 1942, at Fort Devens, Massachusetts. He had completed three years of high school and was employed as a baker. He was born in 1914.

6. The task force sent to Lunéville on September 18 was commanded by Major Hunter of the 37th Tank Battalion. It was comprised of B/53, A/37, and a battery from the 94th Armored Field Artillery Battalion.

7. The name of Sgt. John J. Brown of B/53 appears in the 1995 Christmas issue of *Rolling Together*, the Fourth Armored Division Association's quarterly mailing.

Chapter 8

1. For several days during late September, the Fourth Armored Division engaged several German *Panzer* units in the vicinity of Arracourt, France. It was the largest tank-vs-tank battle during the 1944–45 campaign in western Europe. The 37th Tank Battalion and 704th Tank Destroyer Battalion accounted for more than their fair share of German losses. See Fox, *Patton's Vanguard*—pages 126–168.

2. Per the 53rd AIB Unit Diary, on September 25, Company B dug in at a position one mile north of Juvrecourt. The position is only half a mile south of Moyenvic and overlooks the town.

3. Per the morning report of November 24, Greenockle's field commission had not yet occurred (see note below). His hospital admission report for his injury in July indicates that he had suffered from a wound to the shoulder caused by artillery shell fragments. Treatment was "debridement without closure." He was also diagnosed with "Nasopharyngitis, acute" (i.e., the common cold).

4. T/Sgt. Charles Greenockle appears on the Company B morning report for September 29. The notation indicates he had returned to duty of as September 24. He appears again on November 24 where it is recorded that he was appointed 2nd lieutenant effective November 17. The morning report dated December 13, 1944, reflects that he had by that time

achieved the rank of 1st lieutenant. As of November 24, 1944, he was listed as slightly sick and transferred to a hospital as a non-battle casualty. He was a long-time member of the Fourth, and his name and photo appeared in the Pine Camp book with the rank of sergeant in Company B, 1st Battalion. According to a press report, his wife Dorothy (née Kleeman) was notified that he had been wounded in action on July 19, 1944 (the wound that is referenced in Porter's manuscript). He was born in Brooklyn, New York on February 17, 1917. He attended Hempstead High School and later played professional baseball for several seasons in the American League. Prior to his service, he was employed by the Doubleday Doran company, Garden City. On May 12, 1942, the notice of his marriage license appeared in the *Newsday Nassau Edition*. Charles died in 1990.

5. SNAFU: "Situation Normal All Fucked Up."

Chapter 9

1. According to the 53rd AIB Unit Diary, on October 9, one company per day was sent to Nancy for showers. Company B was the first to go on October 9. On October 14, Company B was authorized to give passes to 20 percent of their men for a day trip to Nancy between the hours of 0700 and 1700. These are the only references in the unit diary relative to Company B personnel being permitted in Nancy. The city was a popular place for those granted leave. The most fortunate of the men were awarded leaves for Paris.

2. Officer Candidate School. As the war progressed, replacement officers were needed in increasing numbers. Replacement officers often arrived fresh out of training and with no combat experience, which did not always sit well with the seasoned combat soldiers they were going to lead.

3. On the Company B morning report for October 18, it is noted that Sergeant Strong was transferred to the hospital as of October 14, "Slightly wounded SIW (self-inflicted wound) dropped from assignment."

4. The morning report for October 29, 1944, states that Private Porter was appointed sergeant as of October 25.

5. According to the battalion diary, on October 19, Company B moved to Saint-Nicolas-de-Port with the mission of guarding the bridges there. They remained on that mission until October 27.

6. According to the 53rd AIB Unit Diary, this occurred on November 2: "At 1330 B Co gave a demonstration in the attack of a fortified area."

7. The link-up between the Third and Seventh U.S. Armies had occurred earlier in the campaign on September 10 (Province, Charles, *Patton's Third Army*, page 42).

Chapter 10

1. According to the 53rd AIB Unit Diary, while the division was in England, Lt. Gen. Patton visited on February 4 and "inspected the area and addressed all officers in the Garrison Theatre at 0900." On May 9 and 10, he observed operations that the 53rd AIB participated in. Following the demonstration, he "spoke to all the officers and men participating in the demonstration, and complimented them very highly on a job well done." "The purpose of the demonstration was to bring out points stressed by General Patton's letter, Subject: "Tactical Use of Separate Tank Battalions," dated 15 April 1944."

2. The 53rd AIB did not assault Château Salins. Porter's account of this attack is likely conflated with another location at another time. On November 12, the 53rd AIB (-A & C Companies) moved into Château Salins with the mission of outposting the town, which had previously been secured by the 26th Infantry Division. On November 16 at 0900 hours, Company B was assigned to relieve Company A, which had been attached to Task Force Hunter (37th Tank Battalion). Company B returned to Château Salins and control of the 53rd AIB at 1700 hours that same day. The 53rd AIB would remain in Château Salins until November 20, all the while attached to Combat Command Reserve.

Notes—Chapter 10

3. On November 13–14, the 53rd AIB Unit Diary notes that Company B reported a mine field, which aligns with Porter's account.

4. At this time, the Fourth Armored Division was operating on the extreme right flank of the Third Army, adjacent to the zone of the U.S. Seventh Army. During the days to come, controversy arose between Major General Wood of the Fourth Armored and Major General Eddy (commanding general of XII Corps, to whom Wood reported). Wood's gambit to move his division into the zone of the Seventh Army became a factor in his eventual relief (Fox, *Patton's Vanguard*, pages 221–232).

5. This was probably a reference to the French First Army, not the Seventh. At the time, elements of the French First Army operated under the command of the 6th Army Group, led by Lt. Gen. Jacob L. Devers (Clarke and Smith, *Riviera to the Rhine*, page 225).

6. Porter was mistaken on the division's objective. At the time, they were advancing north-northeast toward the area of Sarre-Union. Strasbourg is located 35 miles to the southeast of the Fourth Armored Division's location at the time and well within the zone of the U.S. Seventh Army.

7. 1st Lieutenant John A. Gladys is first mentioned in the 53rd AIB Unit Diary on June 6, 1944, when he was appointed one of six "Battalion Soldier Voting Officers." He was with Company B at that time. He appears on the Company B morning report for November 25, where it states he was transferred to a hospital on September 14 and was a "slightly sick non battle casualty dropped from assignment." On the morning report for December 13, 1944, Gladys's status as of September 14 was revised to missing in action. Gladys remained in the Army after World War II and served in both Korea and Vietnam (his highest rank was major). He was born on August 31, 1918, in Stanhope, New Jersey. After graduating from high school, he worked as a supervisor for Western Electric while attending Columbia University. Gladys died on June 17, 2010.

8. Translation: "It is war, my friend, it is war."

9. This is possibly Marcos R. Juarez, who on the morning report for December 5, 1944, is listed as a private. On November 27, 1944, he was lightly injured in action (hit in the forehead and frontal region by artillery fragments) and sent to a hospital. Given his actions as described by Porter, it would not be unreasonable to assume he had been subsequently reduced in rank (though this is not certain). Juarez was wounded by artillery fire again in December. He was one of the older enlisted men, having been born in 1909. He enlisted on March 14, 1942, at Fort Bliss, El Paso, Texas. Prior to his enlistment, he worked as a farmhand and did not advance beyond grammar school.

10. This was most likely Postroff, based upon Porter's description of the terrain.

11. Porter's reference to his age indicates that he was working on the manuscript in 1967.

12. Porter is likely mistaken about this action taking place at Berg. His narrative appears to be a continuation of the assault on Postroff. His description of the approach to the town matches the geography west of Postroff (especially the presence of the stream/river called "Isch").

13. Porter probably witnessed the death of the tank platoon leader Lieutenant William L. Rice, who is listed as being killed in action on December 1, 1944 (American Battle Monuments Commission). However, the date listed by the ABMC is likely inaccurate, as it is documented that Lt. Rice was killed during the attack on Postroff, which occurred on November 25–26 (Irzyk, *Patton's Juggernaut—The Rolling 8 Ball*, page 205). This also lends credence to the assumption that Porter confused Berg with Postroff. As for Lt. Rice, he was a decorated officer of the 8th Tank Battalion, having been awarded the Silver Star and Bronze Star. He had served in combat since Normandy and had been wounded twice, the first time occurring in Brittany and the second on November 11 (Irzyk, *He Rode Up Front for*

Patton, page 174). His tank company was assigned to Task Force Churchill, and it is presumed that Company B of the 53rd AIB constituted the infantry element of the task force. Lt. Rice was born in Bessemer, Michigan in 1917. He was buried at the Lorraine American Cemetery in France.

14. John Rice was treated for an infection that resulted from the wound. He returned to duty.

Chapter 11

1. The Fourth Armored Division had three armored field artillery battalions (AFAB): the 22nd, 66th, and 94th. Each AFAB had 18 M7 self-propelled howitzers which were divided into three batteries of six guns each. The AFAB assigned forward observers to call for support and adjust the fire of the AFAB's howitzers, which placed the observers in the thick of the action.

2. The stream is named "Finnengraben." The bridge and the hill beyond it are easily recognized from a Google street view.

3. Private Max F. Jiminez is listed on the morning report for December 5, 1944, as being slightly sick and transferred to a hospital on November 28. He returned to duty on December 3. He was lightly wounded in action (hit in the buttocks and hip by artillery fire) during the Battle of the Bulge on December 23 and dropped from assignment. He was wounded by artillery fire earlier in the campaign as well (during July 1944). Jiminez was born in 1917 in Arizona. He enlisted on October 20, 1942, while living in Los Angeles, California, where he worked as a groundskeeper.

4. The G-2 is the officer at the division level responsible for military intelligence. Interrogating prisoners was the responsibility of the G-2 and his staff. Lieutenant Colonel Harry E. Brown served as the Fourth Armored Division G-2 throughout the Fourth's time in combat. The same role existed at the regiment and battalion level, but the designation was S-2 to differentiate it from the division staff. The G designation also applied to organizations above the division level (e.g., corps and army).

5. Private Eugene J. Bonvillain. The morning report for December 1, 1944, indicates that Bonvillain was lightly injured in action as of November 25 and transferred to a hospital. He returned to duty on December 2. On the morning report for December 11, it indicates that as of December 6, he was slightly sick, transferred to a hospital, and dropped from assignment. Bonvillain was born in 1922. He lived in Terrebonne County, Louisiana, and completed four years of high school. His enlistment date was June 21, 1943, and he was inducted in New Orleans.

Chapter 12

1. Based upon the description of the terrain, this was very likely the village of Rimsdorf.

2. The village was likely Rimsdorf.

3. The church in Rimsdorf is located at the intersection of Rue Principale and Rue Sainte-Barbe.

4. The operation in the woods east of Rimsdorf occurred on December 2 (53rd AIB Unit Diary).

5. The K Ration was an individual meal that provided between 3000 and 3500 calories. The items were packed in a single carton and came in three versions: breakfast, dinner, and supper (Fox, *Final Battles of Patton's Vanguard*, page 22).

6. On December 4 (the day of this action), the 53rd AIB was paired with the 35th Tank Battalion. The task force was under the command of Major Henry Crosby of the 53rd AIB (source: 35th Tank Battalion after action report).

7. 2nd Lieutenant Walter Farmer. According to the Company B morning report for December 2, 1944, Farmer and 1st Lieutenant Charles L. McKenna were transferred to Company B from the 53rd Armored Infantry Battalion Headquarters as of November 28. As noted on the morning report for January 26, 1945, on January 20, he was among the fortunate to be granted a two-day leave in Paris.

8. The railroad bridge still exists at the time of this writing. The small creek

that it spans is a tributary of the L'Eichel River.

9. Henry A. Crosby is first mentioned in the battalion diary on April 25, 1944. Then a captain in rank, he was assigned to headquarters company and was the senior company commander. As noted on the Headquarters morning report for October 1, 1944, he was promoted to the rank of major as of September 27, 1944, and assigned to the duty of battalion S-3. A career officer, he remained in the Army after the war, rising to the rank of lieutenant colonel in 1950 and eventually retiring at the rank of colonel on November 1, 1963 (source: U.S. Army registers for 1951, 1956 and 1972). He was highly decorated, having been awarded the Silver Star with two oak leaf clusters, the Bronze Star with two oak leaf clusters, and the Purple Heart with three oak leaf clusters. Crosby was born on May 20, 1912, and died of a heart attack on November 1, 1999, in Franconia, NH. He was laid to rest at Arlington National Cemetery, section 59, site 164, along with his wife Letitia (born October 28, 1917, and died December 16, 2006). At the time of his death, he left behind four sons, two daughters, 14 grandchildren, and a sister, Rosalie Crosby Gevers (obituary in the *Boston Globe*, November 4, 1999).

10. As of 2023, the church is St. Gallus-Kirche von Domfessel, located at the intersection of Rue Principale and Rue del l'École.

11. The medic was Private First Class John W. Riley, a native of Illinois born in 1923, who was attached to Company C on November 8, 1944. He was posthumously awarded the Silver Star and Purple Heart. He is interred at the Lorraine American Cemetery, Plot G, Row 6, Grave 14. Special thanks to Erwin Verholen and Reinier Groeneveld for their assistance researching the identity of Pfc. Riley.

12. During the autumn campaign, the use of the M5 light tank for medical evacuation was commonplace. The muddy conditions made it difficult for ambulances and jeeps to perform the task.

13. The stream is called "Lach" and runs north-south through Domfessel.

14. The Company B morning report for December 12, 1944, indicates that Pfc. John Rice and Sergeant Paul S. Porter were both seriously wounded in action, listed as battle casualties, transferred to a hospital, and dropped from assignment as of December 4, 1944.

Epilogue

1. An article in the LaGarde Sentinel, November 1946, described the history of the hospital and announced that the facility would close on November 28 of that year.

2. Copy of letter in possession of Colleen Porter.

3. The date is indicated on Porter's discharge paperwork.

4. The document "Enlisted Record and Report of Separation Honorable Discharge" is in the possession of Colleen Porter.

5. The European-African-Middle Eastern (EAME) Campaign Medal, awarded to those who served in the European Theatre.

6. Paul's first Purple Heart was awarded based upon multiple shrapnel wounds he received on both hands during the fighting near Moyenvic on October 6, 1944. The Oak Leaf Cluster recognized the wound he received on December 4, 1944, at Domfessel.

7. All awards are listed on Porter's discharge paperwork with the separation date of April 21, 1945.

8. This is the address Porter provided on his separation paperwork. We do not know the length of time that transpired between Porter's moving into Palmer's home and his discharge from the Army.

9. Palmer lived with his aunt and uncle at the time of the 1930 census and used that same address and primary contact when he registered for the draft in 1940. In the 1940 census, he was living at another address in St. Louis as a lodger with two other men. On each of these documents, his profession was listed as a salesman for a retail shoe store.

10. 1930 Census information for Palmer.

11. Palmer's employer was identified on his 1940 draft registration card.

Notes—Epilogue

12. Joyce's comments to her daughter Colleen.

13. The ceremony was photographed by Captain A.T. Lawry. Information is drawn from the caption. Sadly, Porter later lost the medal.

14. In an undated 13-page letter to his then ex-wife Joyce and their daughter Colleen, Paul expressed a range of views regarding his faith, with a particular focus on the afterlife. The entire letter was devoted to his religious beliefs.

15. Email from Colleen Porter to Don Fox dated August 21, 2023.

16. Account from Colleen Porter in email to Don Fox dated August 22, 2023.

17. The account of Porter's commitment to the VA hospital comes from Colleen Porter in an email to Don Fox dated August 22, 2023.

18. Fox interview with Colleen Porter.

19. Email from Colleen Porter to Don Fox dated August 22, 2023.

20. The photographs taken near Mount Shasta are dated June 1974.

21. Email from Colleen Porter to Don Fox, August 21, 2023.

22. Paul told this story to Colleen's cousin, Carolyn. Email from Colleen Porter to Don Fox, August 22, 2023.

23. Judgment document rendered in the 24th Judicial District Court, Parish of Jefferson, State of Louisiana.

24. The reference that Paul makes to his age in the manuscript suggests that he had completed his final draft in 1967.

25. The letter from Mr. Hicks to the publisher is in the possession of Colleen Porter. Mr. Hicks had received the manuscript from Mr. Johnie Goines of Fort Smith, Arkansas. We know from this letter that the contact address for Paul at that time was 3826 K Johnson Street, Metairie, Louisiana. This was the address belonging to Colleen's Great Aunt Carrie and where Colleen's family eventually rented a home.

26. Information on Silas's fate is drawn from death certificate E9 55X 67. Silas was buried in Brushy, Oklahoma. His fraternal brother Paul would be buried beside him in 1985.

27. Cancelled check dated October 25, 1978, made out to literary agent Scott Merideth, drawn on Porter's bank in Sallisaw, Oklahoma.

Bibliography

Books

Baldwin, Hanson W. *Tiger Jack*. Ft. Collins, CO: The Old Army Press, 1979.
Belpulsi, Peter A. *A GI's View of World War II*. Salem, Missouri: Globe Publishers, 1997.
Blumenson, Martin. *Breakout and Pursuit—United States Army in World War II: The European Theater of Operation*. Washington, D.C.: Office of the Chief of Military History, 1961.
Blumenson, Martin. *The Duel for France, 1944*. Da Capo Press, 1963.
Boas, Roger. *Battle Rattle: A Last Memoir of WWII*. Stinson Publishing, 2015.
Cole, Hugh M. *The Ardennes: Battle of the Bulge—United States Army in World War II: The European Theater of Operations*. Washington, D.C.: Office of the Chief of Military History, 1965.
Cole, Hugh M. *The Lorraine Campaign—United States Army in World War II: The European Theatre of Operations,* Washington, D.C., Historical Division: Department of the Army, 1950.
Dyer, Lt. Col. George. *XII Corps, Spearhead of Patton's Third Army*. Arcole Publishing, 2017 (originally published 1947).
Eisenhower, Dwight D. *Crusade in Europe*. Garden City, N.Y.: Doubleday, 1948.
Fox, Don M. *Final Battles of Patton's Vanguard—The United States Army Fourth Armored Division, 1945–1946*. Jefferson, North Carolina: McFarland, 2020.
Fox, Don M. *Patton's Vanguard—The United States Army Fourth Armored Division*. Jefferson, North Carolina. McFarland, 2003.
Irzyk, Albin F. *He Rode Up Front for Patton*. Raleigh, North Carolina: Pentland Press, 1996.
Irzyk, Albin F. *Patton's Juggernaut—The Rolling 8-Ball*. Oakland, Oregon: Elderberry Press, 2017.
Koyen, Kenneth. *The Fourth Armored Division—from the Beach to Bavaria*. 1946.
Luciano, Eugene W. *Our Blood and His Guts*. Chapel Hill, NC: Professional Press, 1995.
Patton, George S. *War as I Knew It*. New York, N.Y.: Houghton Mifflin, 1947.
Province, Charles M. *Patton's Third Army—A Chronology of the Third Army Advance, Augusy,1944 to May 1945*. New York, NY: Hippocrene Books, 1992.
Sorley, Lewis. *Thunderbolt—From the Battle of the Bulge to Vietnam and Beyond: General Creighton Abrams and the Army of His Times*. New York: Simon & Schuster, 1992.
Zaloga, Steven J. *Lorraine 1944—Patton vs Manteuffel*. Oxford, UK: Osprey Publishing, 2000.

Papers, Reports, Articles

Gabel, Christopher R., Dr. *The 4th Armored Division in the Encirclement of Nancy*.
Genesis to Greatness 1940–1945. Fourth Armored Division Association, 1982.
The Nancy Bridgehead. Subordinate commanders and staff of Combat Command A, 4th Armored Division, Fort Knox, Kentucky.

Bibliography

Vandergriff, Donald E., Captain, U.S. Army *The Exploitation from the Dieulouard Bridgehead*. ARMOR Magazine, September-October 1995.

Combat Histories, After Action Reports and Interviews

After Action Report 22nd Armored Field Artillery Battalion—July 1944–May 1945 (n.p., n.a.).
After Action Report 53rd Armored Infantry Battalion—July 1944 through May 1945 (n.p., n.a.).
After Action Report 66th Armored F.A. Battalion—July 1944 Thru April 1945.
Battalion Diary: 37th Tank Battalion, 4th Armored Division. By "Unknown Soldier," U.S. Army Command and General Staff College, Fort Leavenworth, Kansas.
Combat Diary of the 94th Armored Field Artillery Battalion 1944–1945 (n.p., n.a.).
Combat History of the 4th Armored Division. 1944–45. U.S. Army Command and General Staff College. Fort Leavenworth, Kansas.
Report After Action against Enemy—Headquarters VIII Corps August 10, 1944. Troy H. Middleton, Major General, U.S. Army, Commanding.
Unit Diary—53rd Armored Infantry Battalion. HQ, 53rd Armored Infantry Battalion.

Index

Numbers in **_bold italics_** indicate pages with illustrations

Abrams, Lt. Col. Creighton 175*n*5, 182*n*6, 184*ch*7*n*3, 184*ch*7*n*4
Albertson, Erik **_69_**
Allen Shoe Company 163, 165, 168
Alsace Lorraine 84, 88, 92, 102, 104, 121, 146
Avranches 53, **_54_**, 56, 60–2, 75, 100, 111, 126, 151, 180*n*1, 180*n*5

Baerendorf **_125_**, 175*Pref(Fox)n*1
Baird, Maj. Gen. Henry Welles 175*n*5
Baker, Col. Sam H. 166, **_168_**
Baltimore 72
Barneville 177*n*1
Bath 19
Berg 123, 175*Pref(Fox)n*1, 186*n*12, 186*n*13
Biloxi 170
Blackie (soldier) 66, 68, 73, 98–100, 159
Blois 72, 74, 183*ch*6*n*1
Blythe 13
Boeck, Sgt. 56, 58, 110–11
Bonvillain, Pvt. Eugene J. 137, 187*ch*11*n*5
Bradley, Lt. Gen. Omar N. 177*n*5
Brittany Peninsula 7, 49, 51, 53, 61, 180*n*2, 181*n*5, 186*n*13
Brown, Sgt. John J. 88–90, 184*n*7
Brushy 11, 174, 176*n*8, 189*n*26

California Desert Training Center 16
Camp Bowie 16–8, 35, **_42_**, 163, 179*ch*2*n*6
Camp Ibis 16
Camp Myles Standish 18
Camp Plauche 166
Capo, Pvt. Charles 57–8, 75–7, 151, 155, 180–1*ch*4*n*8
Cardone, Sgt. Steve J. 25–6, 46, 177*n*2
Château Salins 113–4, 185*ch*10*n*2
Cherbourg 178*n*7

Cobra, Operation 7, 180*ch*3*n*7, 180*ch*3*n*8
Company B, 53rd Armored Infantry Battalion 3, 5, 7, 16, 18–21, **_22_**, 23, 25–6, 31, 45, 48, 55, 67, 139, 161
Company C, 53rd Armored Infantry Battalion 118, 145, 152–4
Coutances 49, 51–2, 180*n*3, 180*n*4
Crosby, Capt. Henry A. 20, 153, 156–9, 187*n*6, 188*ch*12*n*9

Dager, Brig. Gen. Holmes B. 177*n*5, 180*n*3
Devizes 18–20, 145
Distinguished Service Cross (DSC) 4, 5, 8, 161–2, 166, **_168_**, **_169_**, 174, 180*n*3
Domfessel 146, 161, 188*ch*12*n*13, 188*Epi.n*6
Dominico, Sgt. 111
Doss, Pfc. J.P. 33–5, 41, 46, 177*n*2, 179*n*7
Duffy, 2nd Lt. James, Jr. 33–8, 40–1, 46, 73, 178*n*4

Eddy, Maj. Gen. Manton S. **_85_**, 184*ch*7*n*4, 186*n*4
8th Air Force 47, 49
8th Infantry Division 61, 181*n*2
8th Tank Battalion 6, 61, 67, **_120_**, 123, 133, 146, 182*n*7, 186*n*13
80th Infantry Division 83–4, 183*ch*7*n*1, 184*ch*7*n*4
England **_15_**, 18, 28, 46, 96, 114, 118, 145, 146, 161, 178*n*2, 179*n*3, 179*n*5, 185*ch*10*n*1
Eschwiller 175*Pref(Fox)n*1
Eywiller 175 *Pref(Fox)n*1

Farmer, 2nd Lt. Walter 151, 187*n*7
51st Armored Infantry Battalion 16, 176*n*13, 177*n*5

193

Index

53rd Armored Infantry Battalion 1, 3, 5, 7, 16–21, 23, 25–6, **62**, **125**, 161, 177*ch*1*n*16, 177*n*17, 177*n*18, 179*n*1, 179*n*4, 179*n*5, 180*n*4, 182–8
Firebaugh 15
Florence (AZ) 13
Fort Bliss 186*n*9
Fort Knox 16, 101, 142
Fort Smith 172, 189*n*25
Fourth Armored Division 3–8, 16, 18, 29, 49, 83, 102, 130, 136
4th Infantry Division 27–8, 30–1, 46, 177*n*5, 178*n*7
Free Holiness Church 14
Fresno 14–5

Gladys, 1st Lt. John A. 118–9, 121, 186*n*7
Goines, Johnie 175*Pref(Porter)n*1, 189*n*25
Green, Lt. Ivan D. 68–71, 98, 182*n*8
Greenockle, 2nd Lt. Charles 95–6, 184–5*ch*8*n*4
Gross, T/5 Alvin 86, 184*n*5

Hanford 14
Hicks, Ed 172, 175*Pref(Porter)n*1
Hitler, Adolf 29, 30, 178*n*9
Houston 172
HQ Company, 53rd Armored Infantry Battalion 21

Irzyk, Major Albin F. 186*n*13

Jaques, Lt. Col. George L. 16, **17**, 20–1, 176*n*13, 182*n*6
Jiminez, Pvt. Max F. 133–4, 187*ch*11*n*3
Juarez, Sgt. Marcos R. 119–121, 186*n*9

Kelly, T/Sgt. Michael J. 33–4, 178*n*1
Kent, Bosman C. 13
Keyes, Sgt. 105, 107–9
Kiernan, Joe 58–9, 100–1, 181*n*9
Kirrberg 175*Pref(Fox)n*1
Klinkosky, Pfc. Joseph 41–2, 179*n*1
Kolodzieski, Benjamin 155
Kovacs, Pvt. John 43, 55, 89, 91, 179*n*2

LaGarde General Hospital 161, 188*n*1
Loire River 72, 183*ch*6*n*1
London 18, 178*n*4, 179*n*3
Lorient 181*n*5
Louis, Joe (boxer) 20
Luciano, Tech. Sgt. Eugene W. 175*Pref(Fox)n*2

Luftwaffe 53, 180*n*5
Lunéville 88, **89**, 90, 92, 184*n*6
Luxbacher, Lt. John W. 33–4, 36–8, 70, 126, 178*n*2
Lydiard, Millicent 20

MacDonald, Charles B. 9
Marne River 183*ch*7*n*1
Martin, Cecilia Cook **164**, 165
Meredith, Scott 175*Pref(Porter)n*1, 189*n*27
Metairie 170, 175*Pref(Porter)n*1
Meuse River 183*ch*7*n*1
Mince, Albert 171
Morrison, James H. 166, 174
Moselle River 9, 83–4, 183*ch*7*n*1, 184*ch*7*n*3
Moyenvic 92–3, 102, 106, 184*ch*8*n*2, 188*n*6

Nancy 92, 104–5, 111, 113, 129, 184*ch*7*n*3, 185*ch*9*n*1
New Orleans 15, 161, 163–5, 170–1, 187*ch*11*n*5
94th Armored Field Artillery Battalion 177*n*5, 184*n*6, 187*ch*11*n*1
Normandy 1, 5, **21**, 23, 25, 28, **29**, 33, **38**, 44, 47–9, **50**, **62**, 73, 96, 151, 162, 180*ch*3*n*7, 186*n*13

Oakland 14
O'Brien, Capt. Francis J. 33, 38, 41–6, 178*ch*2*n*5
101st Airborne Division 8
Orleans 8

Palmer, Charles Glenn 163, **166**, **167**, 170
Paris (France) 159–60, 187*n*7
Paris (TX) 11
Patton, Lt. Gen. George S. 18, 20, 31, 114, 161, 175*n*5, 185*n*1
Pine Camp 16, 179*n*2, 182*n*8
Porter, Bessie 12, 176*n*1
Porter, Colleen 4, 5, 168–73
Porter, Doris Dean 11–2, 13, 14, **16**, 171, 176*n*1
Porter, Ella Mae 14, 176*n*1
Porter, Ethel 11, 176*n*1
Porter, John B. 11, **12**, 14, 176*n*1
Porter, Joyce Ann Martin 15, 163–4, **165**, **166**, **167**, 168–72, 176*n*1, 189*n*14
Porter, Nora Mae 11–2
Porter, Patricia Mae 23

194

Index

Porter, Paul, Jr. 2, 168, *170*, 171
Porter, Pollie 176n1
Porter, Silas 11, *12*, 14, 173–5, 176n1, 189n26
Porter, Virgie Mae 14, 23
Porter, William, Jr. 11, *12*, 14, *167*, 176n1
Porter, William Monroe Garfield 11, 14, *164*, 176n3, 176n9
Postroff 175*Pref(Fox)*n1, 186n10, 186n12, 186n13
The Preacher (soldier) 25, 27, 46
Prince Maurice Barracks 18

Ramona 14, 23
Rennes 61, 64
Rhine River 8, 74, 102, 113, 114, 117
Rice, Pfc. John J. 72, 90, 125–6, 128, 148–60, 183n2, 187n14, 188n14
Rice, Lt. William L. 126–7, 186n13
Richmond (CA) 15
Riley, Pfc. John W. 188*ch*12n11
Rimsdorf 175*Pref(Fox)*n1, 187*ch*12n1, 187*ch*12n2, 187*ch*12n3, 187*ch*12n4
Riverside 14

Salisbury 20, 177n19
San Joaquin County 13
USAT *Sant Paula* 18, 177n16
Santa Maria 14
Scully, Laura 165, 169–70
Second Armored Division 8, 175*Pref(Porter)*n2, 180*ch*3n8, 182n6
2nd SS Panzer Division 178n8
704th Tank Destroyer Battalion 177n5, 184n1
Seventh Army (German) 49, 54, 180n6
Seventh Army (U.S.) 113, 115
Simonazzi, T/5 Frank, Jr. 62, 64, 116, 181n4
Sixth Armored Division 92, 180n1
66th Armored Field Artillery Battalion 17, *50*, 132, 177n5, 187*ch*11n1
Strasbourg 74, 102, 113, 117, 183n4, 186n6

Strong, Sgt. 97–8, 110–1
Swansea 18

10th Armored Infantry Battalion 16, 45, 175*Pre(Fox)*n2, 176n13, 177n5, 179n4, 183n5
Terrell 172
Third Armored Division 180*ch*3n8, 182n6
Third Army (U.S.) 7, 113, 186n4
13th Infantry Regiment 181n2
35th Evacuation Hospital 181n8, 181n9
35th Tank Battalion 17, 182n7, 183n5, 187n6
37th Tank Battalion 20, 180*ch*4n7, 182n7, 184*ch*7n3, 184*ch*7n6, 184*ch*8n1
Tilshead 20
Troyes 8, 74, 102, 183n5, 183n6
Tulsa 13
12th Evacuation Hospital 181n9
22nd Armored Field Artillery Battalion 6, *30*, *83*, 177n5, 187*ch*11n1
24th Armored Engineer Battalion 6, 18
25th Armored Cavalry Reconnaissance Squadron *59*, 177n5
26th Infantry Division 102–3, 109, 185*ch*10n2

Utah Beach 25, 177n1, 178n6, 178n7

Wanosik, George Joseph "Dutch" (aka the "Polack") 33, 36–8, 41, 43–5, 52–3, 69, 90, 93, 97–8, 111, 124–7, 132–3, 138, 142–3, 152, 178n3
West Point 20, 141, 175n5
Westdown Range 20
Weymouth 23, 177n1
Wood, Maj. Gen. John S. 3, 7, 20, 51, 84, *85*, 175*Pref(Porter)*n2, 175n5, 177n5, 180n3, 181n5, 184*ch*7n4, 186n4
Woodhaven 14
World War II Armor (organization) 26, *52*, *63*
Wuestenhagen, 1st Sgt. Arnold 44, 179n3

www.ingramcontent.com/pod-product-compliance
Ingram Content Group UK Ltd.
Pitfield, Milton Keynes, MK11 3LW, UK
UKHW042008140426
5217IPUK00015B/1056